When Words Collide

A Media Writer's Guide to Grammar and Style

From the Wadsworth Series in Mass Communication and Journalism

NINTH EDITION

When Words Collide

A Media Writer's Guide to Grammar and Style

Lauren Kessler
University of Oregon

Duncan McDonald
University of Oregon

CENGAGE
Learning·

Australia • Brazil • Mexico • Singapore • United Kingdom • United States

CENGAGE
Learning®

When Words Collide, A Media Writer's Guide to Grammar and Style, Ninth Edition

Lauren Kessler and Duncan McDonald

Product Director: Monica Eckman

Product Manager: Kelli Strieby

Content Developer: Kathy Sands-Boehmer

Product Assistant: Rachel Schowalter

Media Developer: Janine Tangney

Marketing Manager: Jillian Borden

Art and Cover Direction, Production Management, and Composition: Carolyn Deacy and Jitendra Kumar, MPS Limited

Manufacturing Planner: Doug Bertke

Text and Cover Designer: Ellen Pettengell

Cover Image: Words: Shutterstock.com

Impact Earth: iStock/Solarseven

Library of Congress Control Number: 2014938526

ISBN: 978-1-285-05247-2

Cengage Learning
20 Channel Center Street
Boston, MA 02210
USA

Cengage Learning is a leading provider of customized learning solutions with office locations around the globe, including Singapore, the United Kingdom, Australia, Mexico, Brazil, and Japan. Locate your local office at **www.cengage.com/global**

Cengage Learning products are represented in Canada by Nelson Education, Ltd.

To learn more about Cengage Learning Solutions, visit **www.cengage.com**

Purchase any of our products at your local college store or at our preferred online store **www.cengagebrain.com**

Printed in the United States of America
Print Number: 01   Print Year: 2014

Contents

Preface

Online, on paper, on the air. Where will your writing appear?

Apps, podcast scripts, blog posts, news bulletins, essays. Speeches, ad copy. Investigative reports, narrative features, video documentaries, multimedia presentations. What will you write?

You may not know yet, and if you do know (and even if you are *very, very* sure), it's more than likely you will change your mind and the direction of your career many times as you grow and change — and as the fast-paced world of communications grows and changes. What will remain, what is at the core of all of these endeavors, all these "delivery systems," all the new and changing technology that will always be a part of our lives is this: correct, crisp, compelling prose. Good, solid writing. Writing that sparks discussion, ignites emotions, captures experience, tells stories. And do you know what is at the core of that? Good grammar. This brings us to the book you hold in your hands. Welcome to the new edition of *When Words Collide*, your friendly (yes, really) and authoritative guide to grammar and word use.

Whether you're a veteran writer or a writer-in-training, a would-be, a wanna-be or a might-be, we welcome you to this book. We also welcome those of you brought kicking and screaming to a book on grammar. However you got here, we're glad to have you. We're glad to share our love of language and our commitment to great writing.

If you want to write well, *When Words Collide* can help you.

There are those who find the study of grammar endlessly fascinating. We wish them well, but we don't number ourselves among them. Rather, we are writers who understand a fundamental concept: The better we know the tools of our trade, the better writers we will be. We don't *love* grammar. We *need* it. We get frustrated, just like you, with its intricacies and inconsistencies, its sometimes finicky rules and occasionally exasperating exceptions. But we know from experience that the reward for mastering grammar is the ability to write with clarity, power and grace. And that means the ability to connect with an audience, to make people think and care—and maybe even laugh.

It is from our perspective as committed writers, avid readers, and (we hope) thoughtful teachers that we offer this ninth edition of *When Words Collide*. We want you to stick with us, read the book carefully and use it as a reference while you write. Learn grammar not for its own sake, not—*please*—to pass some test, but rather because grammar is one of the foundations of good writing.

This is the best *When Words Collide* yet. We—your authors—have continued to grow and to challenge ourselves as writers and teachers. We've tracked, studied and been an active part of the new and ever-evolving world of cross-platform, multimedia journalism. This new edition comes out of our unshakable belief in and passion for the extraordinary power of crisp, clear, compelling prose. You will read, in the first chapter, why *honing language skills is more important in today's media world* than ever before. We think you'll be surprised why this is so. You'll find that we've *simplified grammatical rules and regulations* throughout the book without sacrificing the goal of mastery. You'll find that we talk to you. *We don't lecture or preach.* We talk. We offer *examples from a wide range of work* including song lyrics, advertising copy, blogs and (just for the fun of it) worst-writing-ever contests as well as straight ahead journalism. In this edition we include *boxed material to highlight, illustrate and entertain*. We have also reorganized the grammar workbook so that it correlates more closely to the chapters in the text.

Reading a book about writing should be a pleasure. We hope this one is. We hope this book helps you become the best writer you can be. We hope you keep it on your desk for years to come.

Resources

This text is accompanied by a printed student workbook that features detailed, hands-on exercises designed to reinforce each chapter's key grammar and style concepts. The workbook is available for purchase at www.cengagebrain .com. Instructors can find the answer key to the workbook on the book's Instructor Companion Site, at www.login.cengage.com. If students would like additional practice with the book's grammar and style concepts, tutorial quizzes are available on the Student Companion Site, at www.cengagebrain.com.

Acknowledgments

We thank the following reviewers for their ideas and comments: Bernard Armada, University of St. Thomas; Susan Case, West Virginia University; Catherine Cassara, Bowling Green State University; Frank Coffman, Rock Valley College; Dan Connell, Simmons College; David Dixon, Malone University; Darryl Ewing, University of Houston; Jennifer Follis, University of Illinois; Neal Haldane

Madonna University; Rachel Kovacs, College of Staten Island; Jan Larson, University of Wisconsin–Eau Claire; Kathy Olson, Lehigh University; Syrenthia Robinson, Virginia Tech; Robin Street, University of Mississippi; and Joanne Washington, Clarion University. We especially thank the many teachers around the country who have enthusiastically supported our efforts and have made *When Words Collide* a part of their classes. We thank the thousands of students who have struggled with the complexities of the English language on the road to becoming professional writers. We dedicate this book to them and to our families.

Lauren Kessler

Duncan McDonald

Eugene, Oregon

PART 1

Understanding Grammar and Style

Grammar Lives! 1

Grammar.

I know, right?

If you winced when you read, "I know, right?" (and we hope you did), it's because, although that expression is common in conversation, it is eminently wince-worthy in writing. Actually, it's wince-worthy in conversation too, but that's another matter. The point is, conversation and written expression, though they both use words, phrases and sentences, are very different beasts. We have much higher expectations for written expression—and not just "writerly" writing like the high-class prose found in prize-winning books and "New Yorker" magazine stories.

Clear, concise, focused writing is essential in reports and proposals, in emails and blog posts and, yes, even in tweets. Correct and careful language use not only leads to solid (efficient, meaningful) communication in all of its many forms, it also directly reflects on your character.

Yes, your *character*. By taking the time and the care to use language correctly, you show yourself to be the kind of person who knows the value and importance of taking time and taking care. Your crisp use of language shows you to be a clear and direct thinker, the kind of person someone would like to mentor or hire or promote, the kind of person whose project some organization might want to support and fund.

Is there a secret to writing with clarity and crispness? Is there a key to crafting the kind of powerful yet conversational, information-rich yet occasionally witty writing valued in traditional media, digital media, social media and just about everywhere else? Happily, yes: The key is the mastery of grammar.

But wait a minute. We've all heard and read so much about the gutting of newsrooms and the demise of traditional book publishing and the increasingly fickle world of magazines. We've been deluged with reports about how *social* media is more important than media, about how "citizen journalists" are usurping the duties of *journalist* journalists and how this thing we call journalism is gasping its last breath. Given all this, how important is writing well anyway? Do we really need to study and perfect our use of words?

In a word: Yes.

In fact, now more than ever.

Let us explain. We (that is, the trustworthy, hardworking, media-savvy authors of the book you are reading) would like you to consider these three compelling reasons that mastery of grammar and word use is more important and more relevant today than ever before.

Why Grammar is More Important Than Ever

1. **Learned disregard for correct word use.** An entire generation— yours—has grown up using words in ways past generations have not. You write more in your personal life than your parents or their parents did (although perhaps less in your academic life). Texting, messaging, tweeting, posting updates: You use the written word where past generations used the spoken word. That is, they gabbed and gossiped face to face and on the phone. For them, casual communication between friends meshed nicely with the casual way we use speech, the *I know, right?* construction.

   But consider what can happen when we consistently use the written word to communicate immediate, off-hand remarks, when most of our daily practice in written communication is in dashing off super-casual quips and comments. Here's what happens: an erosion of, even a disregard for, the niceties of language. When you're in a hurry, when the communication is taking place between people who know each other, when the stakes are pretty low—all those factors conspire against careful construction, correct grammar and precise wording.

   They are almost never priorities—or even considerations. That's probably just fine for casual communication. But if you're serious about a career in any field that involves writing (which is just about every field, from journalism and communications to law and business), you are faced with this challenge: Learn to distinguish between how you are accustomed to using written language to communicate casually from how you must learn to use written language to communicate publicly and professionally.

2. **The culture of traditional journalism versus the culture of online journalism.** There's a clash of cultures going on right now between the embedded, time-honored values of traditional journalism and the newer,

emerging values of today's uber-mediated world. People have been talking and writing about this clash of cultures for years, mostly from the point of view of economics and, more recently, ethics. But there's also a clash in the trenches, where journalism is reported, written and produced.

Traditional journalism has long depended on the "luxury" of time—the need to produce only *one* newspaper a day, *one* evening broadcast, *one* magazine a month—and sizable trained staff to oversee the creation and crafting of material. This careful crafting depends on time to report, write, edit, revise and rewrite. But in the new world of journalism, time has been redefined. Or obliterated. The news cycle is 24/7. Reports and images zip around the globe almost instantaneously via social media. The Pope tweets. Immediacy is the core value.

Amid this often frantic activity and the rush to get out news and information at lightning speed, attention to correct, concise word use and clear, grammatical construction may seem like a luxury. It isn't. Given the constant bombardment of information, it is even more of a necessity.

Also, let's face it: The barriers to publishing work on the Web are much lower (almost nonexistent) compared to publishing work in traditional media. Hooray for low barriers when it comes to expanding ideas and including diverse voices and views! But low barriers also mean nominal—or no—expectations for correct, concise, powerful language use. You quickly learn that, in terms of written expression, you can get away with almost anything on the Web. This is not a lesson to take to heart.

3. **The decline and fall of editing.** It used to be that a grammatically challenged journalist could count on—not to mention fear—the long arm (and keen eye) of an editor. Editors, from section editors to departmental editors, to copy editors, to proofreaders would comb through the journalist's prose for clutter and clunkiness, for weak word choice, for misplaced modifiers and lack of parallelism and for errors of both fact and usage. But at today's struggling newspapers, buyouts and layoffs have vastly reduced the number of editors on staff. In the musical-chairs worlds of magazine and book publishing, editors come and go with dizzying regularity. Increasingly, it is difficult to find an experienced, long-time editor who has both the time (now that there are so few of them) and the expertise to make weak prose strong.

Veteran journalist and University of Maryland Professor Carl Session Stepp calls this the "quality-control quandary." Quality control as it relates to the accuracy and veracity of information and the correctness of language use is an issue—a big issue. The safety net in terms of catching and fixing poor, incorrect or otherwise flabby language use is either nonexistent (on the Web) or disappearing (in traditional media). Guess what? That means it is up to us—journalists, writers, communicators, creators of content—to step it up. Now is absolutely the time to commit to mastering the tools of the trade.

You don't have to wait for an assignment in class. You can start right now. You can start close to home, with email and your personal media habits.

What Does Your Email Say About You?

Compared with texting and messaging, email seems old fashioned, stodgy even. Although not as impossibly quaint as an actual letter placed in an actual envelope and deposited in an actual mailbox, email is nonetheless comparatively prim and proper. You may have moved away from email as a primary means of communicating with friends, but you should know that close to 2.5 billion people use email worldwide and that on an average day these folks send about 150 billion emails. Email is vital to global communications, commerce and conversation.

Emailers spend far more time (and use more words) constructing messages than texters. They are more likely than texters to write in full sentences and less likely to use shortcuts (b4, gr8), abbreviations (lol) or contractions that may, with enough use, confound correct spelling (thx, ur). Adhering to grammatical conventions makes sense because email is, in fact, more formal than texting. It is an integral part of the business and professional world.

Dependence on email in the workplace combined with its limbo-land status—less formal than the business letters or memos of old, more formal than friend-to-friend texting—is creating big problems, say those in the business world. In a lengthy story on the subject in "The Wall Street Journal," the headline of which read "Thx for the IView! I Wud (heart) to Work 4 U!!," recruiters and personnel managers railed against too casual communication. One national recruiter quoted in the story said that she had interviewed a particular candidate and thought she had found the perfect intern until she received the candidate's thank-you email. It was laced with words like "hiya" and "thanx" along with three exclamation points and a smiley face. The candidate did not get the job. What some think of as "casual," business people think of as *unprofessional.*

The laid-back, offhand (choose your adjective), short-cut way of communicating that many millions of us use everyday is, when used in the workplace, considered a mark of immaturity and thoughtlessness, an indicator of a more generalized slapdash attitude. (As a related issue, you might want to consider—or reconsider—your email address, which should be straightforward and professional, not the cute, quirky one you created for yourself when you were in middle school.)

Other emails, according to the consultants and writing coaches in the corporate trenches, are just the opposite: inflated and flabby, stuffed with polysyllabic words, cluttered phrasing and tortured sentence structure. And then there are the incoherent emails whose meaning eludes—or, worse, misguides—their receivers. These emails are riddled with incorrect punctuation, misplaced or dangling modifiers, incorrect word choice or syntax so tangled that it would take a machete to cut through it. The grammar—or lack thereof—prevents people from understanding one another.

The lessons to be learned from the corporate experience are important ones. The first one, of course, is that clear written communication matters—not just for those in the communication business but for everyone in the world of work. The second is that the cavalier attitude toward grammatical conventions that comes from, and is daily reinforced by, texting, messaging and posting quirky updates is decidedly not the attitude a media writer (or any working professional) should adopt. And here's a third lesson we'll just throw in: *Just because you can type fast doesn't mean you should write fast.*

Beware the Media Multitasker

We'd like to offer this final idea as you navigate the terrain between casual and professional communication: Media multitasking may be dangerous to your (professional) health—and most certainly to your growth as a writer.

In high school or college you may have become accustomed to media overload. You message a friend while listening to music, doing a homework assignment and checking out a cat video on YouTube. You hop between Facebook and Craigslist (maybe Zappos too? Admit it!) while texting. That may work for you, or you may *think* it works for you, but now that you're on the road to becoming a writer, it's time to reconsider. Decades of research have shown that the more tasks multitaskers attempt, the worse they do at them. An eye-opening Stanford university study of more than 250 college undergrads reinforced this conclusion, finding that the more media multitaskers used, the poorer their performance. Memory, ability to focus and ability to switch between tasks all suffered—mightily.

In fact, brain research shows that there is no such thing as multitasking. The brain cannot do two tasks simultaneously, unless one is what researchers call a "highly practiced skill." That means—not to worry—you *can* walk and chew gum at the same time. But the brain cannot simultaneously perform tasks that require focus, like writing, reading or carrying on a conversation. Instead, a kind of toggle mechanism allows the brain to switch from one activity to another. You may think you are talking to a friend and checking out a website simultaneously, but your brain is really switching rapidly between one activity and the other.

The bad news? When you try to perform two or more related tasks, either at the same time or alternating quickly between them, you not only make far more errors than you would if you concentrated on each task individually, but you actually take far longer (as much as double the time) to complete the jobs than if you had focused on each in sequence. Multitasking is not a time saver; it's a time waster.

Learning to use language correctly, crisply, gracefully, powerfully—which is what this book is about—takes focus and concentration. Our advice: Regardless of the habits you may have developed, when it comes to writing, become a *uni-tasker*.

We hope we've been persuasive in this first chapter. We hope we've given you sensible, realistic—and compelling—reasons to care about the quality of your language use. Your attention to this book, and the energy and focus you decide to devote to mastering grammar, depend on your belief in the power of written expression. We need you to understand how important it is to be skillful in your use of written language. It is important to your success in your career—*in having a career in the first place*—and it is vital to the health and welfare of writing in all its forms.

And it's in your hands.

For additional resources go to **www.cengagebrain.com**

Ten Little Secrets, Ten Big Mistakes   2

Here's what grammar is not: It is not a palette of precepts produced to perplex. It is not a catalogue of caveats created to confuse. It is not a docket of dogma designed to discombobulate. (This is fun! Let's do one more.) It is not a litany of lessons to be listlessly learned. No! Grammar is the essence of good, clear, powerful (occasionally, appropriately jocular) writing. It is the all-important instruction manual that will help you master the tools of the writer's trade: words, phrases, sentences, paragraphs. It is, believe it or not, the key to writing everything from a pithy 140-character tweet to a memorable 140-word blog post, to a compelling 140-page novella.

We're not saying that knowing grammar will automatically transform you into a great writer any more than knowing how to read a script will transform you into Jennifer Lawrence. We are saying that fundamentals underlie the process, both the craft and the art of doing most anything. We are saying that there can be no craft, no art, without the fundamentals. We are saying that a broader focus on the worthy goal of writing well gives meaning to learning the fundamentals. With that in mind, let's focus for a moment on writing and what it takes to write well.

The 10 Secrets of Writing Well

Are there really 10 secrets to writing well? Not likely. Search the Web for "the secret to good writing," and in less than quarter of a second you'll get "about" 517,000,000 results that range from Ernest Hemingway's tough-love approach ("There's nothing to writing. All you do is sit at a typewriter and bleed.") to Marge Piercy's marching orders ("A real writer is one who really writes.")

But maybe there is only one secret: Write. And keep writing. Or is that two? Surely there is more specific helpful advice. Here it is.

Secret #1: Read

"If you don't have time to read, you don't have the time to write." Stephen King wrote that, and you'll get no argument from us.

Reading is not just a way to find out about the world, or yourself; it is an immersion in language. Whether you read a microbiology textbook or a murder mystery, a science blog or a sci-fi story, you are swimming in words, awash in sentences, carried along by a stream of paragraphs. Whether you know it or not, you are learning language along with whatever else you are reading. You are learning vocabulary and syntax, words and how they are put together. You are learning how language flows (or doesn't).

The lessons can be positive and obvious, as when you marvel at a passage that transports you to another time or place, or when, mid-paragraph, you feel in the grip of ideas or emotions. That's a writer forging a connection with words, and it's a lesson you take with you, consciously or not. The more you read, the more you have these experiences, and the more embedded becomes the beauty and the precision of language.

Of course, the lessons can be negative as well—the book that puts you to sleep (not this one, of course), the news story you don't scroll down to finish reading. You are learning something here too: You are learning what doesn't work, how not to put words together, how not to tell a story.

Imagine wanting to be a musician and not listening to music. That's as odd and wrongheaded as aspiring to be a writer and not reading.

Secret #2: Have Something to Say

That sounds too obvious, doesn't it? But how many times have you sat in front of a screen, mind numb, unable to write a single intelligent sentence? You tell yourself you have writer's block. You don't have writer's block. You are more likely suffering from a dearth of material, a paucity of ideas—the lack of something to say. Perhaps you haven't worked your ideas through in your head. You aren't clear about what you think. Or maybe you haven't done the necessary research. You don't know your subject well enough yet. You can't write well if you are not in command of the material. A great writer is smarter than his or her material. A great writer writes from a place of knowing. Simply put: You can't write well if you don't know what you want to say.

Consider how all of us, at times, are reduced to babbling. Sometimes our lips seem to be moving faster than our brains. Words come out. We sputter, stop and start, ramble, backtrack, circumlocute. The lips keep moving, but there is little sense and less meaning behind the words because we haven't stopped to figure out what we want to say. Friends may indulge us, but readers don't.

It's hard to lose a reader if you're tweeting 140 characters. But if you don't have something to say—and you're not Beyoncé, Bieber or the Pope—you're not going to snare, and keep, many followers.

Secret #3: Organize Your Thoughts

Without a plan, writing well is much more difficult than it needs to be. It is not, however, impossible. You can write without a plan if you want to rewrite and revise and restructure many times over. But it is much more sensible, more efficient and decidedly less stressful to think about how you will structure the piece—whatever its purpose or platform—before you begin writing. Some forms of writing have their own internal structure and provide a kind of template you can use. Basic news stories are like that. So are press releases. Advertising copy also often follows a certain pattern. Personal essays conform to a common shape. But even if the template is provided, you need to organize your thoughts and your material within it. And so, determined to write well, you sit with the material, review everything, scribble notes to yourself, look up missing details, check a few more sites, make a few phone calls. You don't rush to write. You take the time to understand the material. From that understanding can come good ideas about how to structure the piece.

You would think this might be a useful advice for longer pieces only. How much planning and structuring are necessary, after all, to write a 300-word blog post? One of your authors blogs regularly at three sites, and she will tell you: a lot. It is harder to write short than long. There's a famous quote about this, at various times and in various places attributed to Benjamin Franklin, Henry David Thoreau, Mark Twain, George Bernard Shaw, Voltaire, Pascal, Winston Churchill, Woodrow Wilson and Bill Clinton: "If I had more time, I would have written a shorter letter." (Pascal, a French mathematician, inventor and writer, said it first.) What he—and all who repeated it later—meant is that writing short involves planning, focusing, organizing and editing. The fewer words you have to work with, the more intensive (and time consuming) the process.

Secret #4: Consider Your Audience

Unlike your tweets or the texts you send to friends, media messages are meant for public consumption. But what public? How can you write well if you don't know who will be reading or listening? You can't—or at the very least you stack the deck against it. If you don't know the audience, you are not sure what your readers or viewers or listeners know or need to know. You are not sure how to approach these folks, what level of vocabulary to employ, what tone to choose, how to structure what you want to say. Should you use humor? Is word play appropriate? Will irony work? Who knows—if you don't know your audience.

That's why companies fund market research: to see who is out there and how best to reach them. That's why magazines conduct readership studies or run surveys to gauge what their readers think about certain issues. That's why serious bloggers track their readers using various diagnostic tools. That's why Facebook knows more about you than your mother. Knowing the audience is a key to good writing.

Secret #5: Know Grammatical Conventions and How to Use Them

Here we are, back to the fundamentals. Note that knowing grammar becomes important only when you have something to say, have figured out how you're going to say it, and know to whom you're talking. The rules themselves—memorizing verb forms or knowing when to use a comma—don't exist without a context. The context is writing. You learn the rules for one reason: to play the game. It's worth noting, for those of you squirming at our repeated mentions of rules, that knowing the rules does allow you to break them (when appropriate, for effect). Breaking a rule on purpose can be creative, artful and entertaining. There is, however, a word for breaking a rule you didn't even know existed, and it is "error."

Writing well means making countless good decisions, from choosing just the right word (see #6) to crafting phrases and clauses and sentences and paragraphs that say just what you want them to say, with precision, clarity and grace (see #7). This lofty but achievable goal is possible only if you understand the architecture of language, the building blocks of prose; if you are at ease with the tools of the trade. Imagine a carpenter who can't use a skill saw, a dancer who doesn't know the steps, a programmer who can't write code. That's a writer without a command of grammar.

Secret #6: Master a Solid Working Vocabulary

Sculptors have clay; painters have paint; writers have words. It's as simple as that. Writers have to figure out how to connect with an audience—spur thought, evoke emotion, inform, educate, entertain, tell a story, set a scene, promote a product, sell an idea—and all they have are words. Yes, words can and do exist within a rich multimedia context. And of course sound and image matter. But what the writer has control of, what the writer revels in, are words. Words are some of the most potent tools around, perhaps the most potent. (Remember the saying "The pen is mightier than the sword"?)

Words carry not only meaning but shades of meaning. What variety, what nuance, what tone! Look up "talk" in a thesaurus and you will find "chatter," "mutter," "mumble," "gossip" and "schmooze," each with its own connotation, each with its own feel. And words not only have meaning and nuance but also sound and rhythm.

Building a good vocabulary means reading widely. It means both appreciating the smorgasbord that is the English language and learning to use words with proper respect. It means choosing the correct word, the word that means exactly what you mean, and spelling it correctly. Building a vocabulary does not mean seeking out multisyllabic tongue twisters or collecting fancy or elaborate expressions. It means being able to use words like "chatter," "mutter," "mumble," "gossip" and "schmooze" when called for.

Secret #7: Focus on Precision and Clarity

If you think clear, crisp writing just flows naturally from fingertips to screen, you couldn't be more wrong. Good writing (even bad writing) doesn't just happen. Regardless of comments like "the story just wrote itself," believe us, stories do not write themselves. Writing with precision and clarity—saying exactly what you mean, no fuzziness, no confusion, no second or third reading necessary—is hard, purposeful work. But it's work your readers, viewers or listeners expect you to do. If you don't, they are a click away from forgetting you ever existed.

Clear, powerful writing is the result of good decisions, from choosing the right word to crafting just the right construction, to relentlessly slashing clutter from your prose. Redundancies? Euphemisms? Jargon? These are obstacles to precision. Misplaced modifiers? Split constructions? Run-on sentences? These are the enemies of clarity. In fact, every grammatical decision you make either enhances or detracts from clarity. That's how important a working knowledge of grammar is to writing well.

Secret #8: Hear Language

"Write for the ear," scriptwriters, podcasters and broadcasters are told, but this is good advice for all writers. It doesn't matter whether the audience actually hears aloud the words you write or just "hears" your prose when reading silently. In either case, the audience attends to the sound and feels the beat. If you can master the skill of writing for the ear, you are one step closer to writing well.

Listen to the words you use. What meaning is conveyed by their sound? Listen to how words sound together. Do they fight one another? Do they flow? Say your written sentences out loud. Do they have a rhythm? A long sentence can lilt. A short sentence can tap out a staccato beat. Purposeful repetition of words or phrases can add rhythm, as can the emphatic use of parallel structure. Experimenting with and eventually mastering the aural nuances and subtleties of language is one of the joys of writing.

Secret #9: Revise

Think you're finished once you write it down? Think all you have to do is a quick once-over, a spell check, and it's out the door? Maybe ... if you're tweeting from an event in real time or pushing out urgent material in a 24/7 news cycle. But most writing is not like that. Most writing, from stories to scripts, blog posts to press releases, demand more than that. They demand revision. Having the patience and fortitude—and humility—to really revise is what separates the amateurs from the professionals. Revision is much more than tidying up, pruning and polishing prose. It is an opportunity to see whether the writing works. It is a chance to rethink what you are trying to say. Consider the word "revision": re-vision means to look again, to look with new eyes. This is what the revision process should be.

And so thoughtful writers, determined to produce clear, powerful, even memorable prose, take a deep breath after they have "finished" whatever it is they were writing. Now it is time to look at the piece and ask: Does it say what I intended it to say? Will my readers or viewers or listeners learn what I want them to learn? Have I written enough or too much? Do the ideas flow from one to another? Do my transitions work? Does my style fit both the subject and the audience? Taking revision seriously means asking the tough questions and being prepared to spend the extra time to answer them.

Even with the best intentions, it is very difficult to learn the art of revision on your own work. You know what you mean even if you don't write what you mean. Thus, when you read your own work, you read what you know

---

Getting it right

We love this snippet from an interview with Ernest Hemingway, the iconic American novelist who began his career as a journalist:

Interviewer: How much rewriting do you do?

Hemingway: It depends. I rewrote the ending of "Farewell to Arms," the last page of it, thirty-nine times before I was satisfied.

Interviewer: Was there some technical problem there? What was it that had stumped you?

Hemingway: Getting the words right.

you meant and not necessarily what you have written. A talented and patient editor can help you see what you have and have not accomplished. If you are lucky enough to find one, be attentive, be humble and sponge up all you can.

Secret #10: Apply the Seat of the Pants to the Seat of the Chair

The final secret to writing well is the easiest to state and the hardest to accomplish: Put in the time. Just like mastering a musical instrument or a new sport, learning to write takes practice—lots of practice. This means time—good, concentrated, focused time over weeks and months and, yes, even years. Some people have a natural facility with words (probably because they are voracious readers). Others struggle. But everyone who wants to write well, talent notwithstanding, has to work hard at it. It is easy to get discouraged. It is easy to get distracted. It is *very* easy to get distracted. Multi-tasking and writing are wildly incompatible. Writing as a uni-tasker is hard enough.

Grammar is Everywhere

We wanted to make the case for writing before we got serious about making the case for grammar. We wanted you to have a reason to care about grammar. You don't have to feel warm and fuzzy about it. You don't have to join a grammar Facebook fan page. But you do have to attend to it. You do have to master it if you want to write well. The good news is that grammar is not rocket science. True, the English language can be challenging. And yes, there is much to learn on the way to mastering the rules that govern how we write. But there is no reason to be intimidated. We human beings are prewired to do this kind of work. Communication is our claim to fame, evolutionarily speaking. We're good at this. It's just that those of us who want to be writers have to be *very* good at this.

That's where grammar comes in. Grammar makes communication possible. Without the shared conventions of grammar, without the structure it creates and the patterns it plots, we could not speak to one another across time and space. Grammar binds us together whether we write status updates or serious journalism, blogs or bestsellers; whether we are veterans of the craft or mere beginners.

We know that grammar has a bad rap: It's confusing. It's picky. It's fussy. There are almost as many exceptions as there are rules. And it's, well, unnecessary, isn't it? "I never learned grammar in school, but it hasn't hurt me yet," you say. "I don't bother with grammar when I text, and no one seems to care—or even notice. Besides," you say, "I can always write around what I don't know. It's the ideas that count, not the grammar."

Sorry. Wrong on all counts.

First of all, grammar is not all that confusing. In fact, it is mostly logical and orderly, often commonsensical and very accessible (that's right: not rocket science). Most of the rules are straightforward, and, happily, good grammar almost always sounds right to those who read and have the patterns of prose embedded in their brains. Second, grammar is absolutely necessary, not only to writing clearly but also to writing with style, creativity and pizzazz.

On this subject we never tire of quoting Joan Didion, journalist, essayist, novelist, memoirist, screenwriter and one of the finest modern prose stylists: "All I know about grammar is its infinite power," she writes. "To shift the structure of a sentence alters the meaning of that sentence, as definitely and inflexibly as the position of a camera alters the meaning of the object photographed. Many people know about cameras today, but not so many know about sentences."

But we must know about sentences, about phrases, clauses, voices, tenses, singulars, plurals—all the patterns and constructions that make our language work. Language is how we spread ideas and information throughout society. The information we have to communicate as writers may be complex; the ideas may be challenging. The message will have to compete with countless distractions for the attention of the audience. It may even have to compete with its own format in multimedia presentations. This puts a tremendous burden on the language: It must be crisp and clear, easy to understand and inviting. It must carry the ideas effortlessly, even gracefully. It must enhance meaning. It must communicate tone and nuance, color and texture, sound and rhythm. But to do all this, the language must be—before all else—correct. It must be grammatical.

Making Mistakes

Learning to write well—and beyond that, to write compellingly, evocatively, gracefully—is a lifelong process. That's the challenge, and it only gets more interesting (and more challenging) the longer we do it. Throughout our lives as writers, we will grow; we will change; and, inevitably, we will make mistakes: judgments miscalled, questions unasked and language misused. Errors can be disheartening, not to mention embarrassing. (Egregious errors like fabricating facts, manufacturing sources or misrepresenting yourself can, and should, be career ending.)

Grammatical errors are particularly hazardous to the health of wannabe writers. "If I see a misspelled word on a résumé or a grammatical error, I look no further. I immediately disqualify the applicant," says the personnel director of a large company. "We look at how much attention a person pays to detail," says the vice president of a major advertising firm. "Things like grammar, spelling and mechanics mean a lot to us. We figure, if the person can't accomplish these things, how can we expect him or her to move on to bigger jobs?" Says an online editor: "If a person can't use grammar correctly, it says either of two things to me—lack of intelligence or extreme sloppiness. Either way, it's not the person I want writing for me." A magazine editor agrees: "We get hundreds of email queries from writers proposing stories for us. For some reason, people think it's okay to write poorly when they write an email. We don't think so at all. We would never hire a freelance writer if that person emailed us a query with grammatical or spelling errors. And it's amazing how many of them do."

But mistakes do happen. It is precisely because professional writers know this—and understand the unpleasant consequences of making errors publicly—that they take editing (and editors) so seriously. Misspelled words, misplaced modifiers, lack of parallelism, shifts in voice—all the little errors that can creep into writing never make it past the editing process. It is during this process that experienced writers turn their uncertain, sometimes ragged prose into the polished material they can proudly present to their audience.

What You Don't Know ...

You know the expression "What you don't know won't hurt you"? Forget it. What you don't know *will* hurt you when it comes to grammar. What you don't know will hurt the clarity of your writing, the understanding and respect of your audience, even your ability to land a job in the first place. What is it you don't know? Let's consider 10 of the most common grammatical mistakes and how knowledge of the language (and reading this book) can help you avoid them.

Mistake #1: Thinking You Don't Have to Know Grammar to Write Well

After reading our masterfully persuasive arguments in these beginning chapters, you're not likely to make this mistake again, right?

Mistake #2: Subjects and Verbs that Don't Agree

For a sentence to be grammatically correct and clearly communicative, a verb must agree with the intended number of its subject. That sounds simple, as in: *The laptop* [singular subject] *is* [singular verb] *on sale* or *The laptops* [plural subject] *are* [plural verb] *in the store*. But it gets complicated when you're not quite sure what the subject is. There may be a number of nouns and pronouns in the sentence. Which is the true subject? *A box of books are/is on the table*. Is *box* (singular) the subject, or is *books* (plural)? There may be confusion about the intended number of the subject. "Five thousand dollars," as a subject, looks plural but acts singular; "everyone," as a subject, clearly implies the plural but acts as a singular subject. To sort this all out, you need to know the parts of speech (Chapters 4 and 5), the parts of a sentence (Chapter 3) and the guidelines for agreement (Chapter 6).

Mistake #3: Subjects and Pronouns that Don't Agree

To communicate crisply and clearly, sentences must have internal harmony. Just as subjects and verbs must agree, so too must subjects and their pronouns. It's a simple rule that depends on your ability to identify the subject, recognize its number and choose a corresponding pronoun. This can be easy, as in: *The musicians* [plural subject] *and their* [plural pronoun] *fans*. Or it can be tougher, as in: *The band made* (their/its) *way to the stage*. But if you understand the parts of speech (Chapters 4 and 5) and the guidelines for agreement (Chapter 6), you should be able to avoid this pitfall.

Mistake #4: Lack of Parallelism

To be both coherent and forceful, a sentence must have parallel structure; that is, its elements must be symmetrical. Consider a construction like *I came. I saw. I conquered*. It is powerful because it sets out three ideas in three parallel grammatical structures (pronoun–past-tense verb). Consider the same idea expressed this way: *I came. I looked over everything. The enemy was conquered by my armies*. That's lack of parallelism. That's startlingly poor writing. You have to know the parts of speech (Chapters 4 and 5) to understand the concept of parallelism, and you must see parallelism as a form of agreement (Chapter 6), as vital to clarity (Chapter 8) and even as an element of style (Chapter 9).

Mistake #5: Confusing *Who* and *Whom*

Who/whom *did the journalist contact first? She worked for* whoever/whomever *could afford her fee. The blogger* who/whom *broke the story refused to reveal his sources*. Confused? You won't be once you understand the nominative and objective cases (Chapter 6).

Mistake #6: Confusing "That" and "Which"

Did you think these two words were interchangeable? Well, they aren't. Consider this sentence: *The full-body scan* that/which *the doctor recommended showed no abnormalities.* "That" is used to introduce material that restricts the meaning of the noun; "which" is used to elaborate on meaning. If you know about relative pronouns (Chapter 5) and the role of phrases and clauses in a sentence (Chapter 3), you will use these words correctly.

Mistake #7: Confusing Possessives and Contractions

That's a fancy way of saying that "your" (possessive) and "you're" (contraction) are not interchangeable. They perform very different tasks in a sentence. "Their" and "they're," "whose" and "who's," "its" and "it's" may sound the same, but they have decidedly different grammatical functions. If you text, you're probably accustomed to omitting apostrophes. Some smartphones insert apostrophes—sometimes incorrectly—themselves. You may also be accustomed to shortcuts: "yr" for "your" (possessive) or "ur" for "you're" (contraction). These are habits you'll have to break (Chapter 1). Learning parts of speech (Chapter 4 and 5) and case (Chapter 6) will help you make the distinction between possessive and contractions, and end the confusion.

Mistake #8: Dangling and Misplaced Modifiers

A misplaced modifier (a word, phrase or clause) does not point clearly and directly to what it is supposed to modify. A modifier "dangles" when what it is supposed to modify is not part of the sentence. Both grammatical errors seriously compromise clarity of meaning. If you understand parts of speech (Chapters 4 and 5) and parts of the sentence (Chapter 3), this clarity, conciseness and coherence issue (Chapter 8) will make sense.

Mistake #9: Misusing Commas

Some novice writers liberally sprinkle their sentences with commas as if this important punctuation mark were a decorative tweak. Tweeters, texters and instant chatters, on the other hand, often eschew commas entirely. But commas have specific functions in a sentence, as do all marks of punctuation. Two specific errors stand out: One is neglecting to use a comma to separate two independent clauses linked by a coordinating conjunction. The other is using only a comma when trying to link two independent clauses (known as the comma-splice error). If some of this terminology is foreign to you, it won't be after you read about parts of speech (Chapter 5), the sentence (Chapter 3) and punctuation (Chapter 7).

Mistake #10: The Dreaded Passive Voice

Passive voice is one of the surest ways to suck the life out of a sentence, a one-way ticket to stilted, falsely formal or bureaucratic prose. Although passive voice construction is not technically a grammatical error and although there are a few defensible reasons for using it, most passive-voice sentences are not written knowingly or purposefully. Both the clarity (Chapter 8) and the liveliness (Chapter 9) of writing are at stake.

All these grammatical hazards—we could list dozens more—may seem daunting. Don't be daunted. Be respectful. Understand that language is alive, complex, fascinating—and full of potential pitfalls. That doesn't mean you should be intimidated. It means you should be careful. It means you should learn the tools of your trade. It means you should study the fundamentals and build your writing from this firm foundation. "When Words Collide" can help.

As you read, never forget that the point of grammar is not grammar. The point is writing well. Please don't lose sight of why you're learning grammar—and why you're reading this book.

The study of grammar is the key to the power of words.

Read on.

Write on.

For additional resources go to **www.cengagebrain.com**

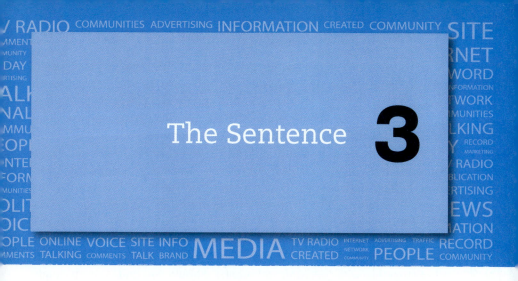

Don't fire until you see the whites of their eyes.

Behold the power of the sentence, the simple, purposeful, potent ordering of words that can change history. Now imagine how fuzzy, clumsy, cluttered, stumbling language could easily rob that masterful sentence of its force:

Don't fire your weapons at the approaching enemy until they are very close to you and you can almost make out their facial features.

Of course the Revolutionary War Army officer (historians can't agree on his identity) who delivered the famous "whites of their eyes" command would never have uttered a shambling, rambling sentence like the one we created. Why not? Was it because he had read a grammar book? Probably not. It was because he had to communicate quickly, clearly and powerfully. His message needed to be direct and forceful and leave no room for misinterpretation. Wait a minute ... doesn't this sound just like the job of the media writer?

Few of us write (or speak) sentences as memorable as the one that began this chapter, but all good writers work hard to craft their words into meaningful constructions that connect with readers. The sentence is the essential building block of memorable prose. To write it well is to know it well.

Learning how to construct a truly worthy sentence—grammatical and graceful, lively and memorable—is a challenge. But learning the basics is not. After all, we *know* sentences. We say them silently to ourselves and out loud to our friends. We text and tweet them. We scribble them on sticky notes. However, when it comes to studying exactly how sentences are created, it's easy to feel so overwhelmed with definitions, exceptions, rules and regulations that we forget we are already experts.

If you see unfamiliar grammatical terms in this chapter, don't panic. In the chapters following this one, you will learn all you need to know (well, almost) about parts of speech, the individual building blocks of sentences. Here, in this chapter, we wanted to give you a reason to *care* about these building blocks—and that reason is the sentence.

You will be reading about all kinds of sentences: simple, compound, complex, compound–complex, incomplete, run-on, subordinated, over-subordinated, passive voice. Don't be put off by these descriptors, and don't obsess about them either. Just think of them as shorthand or code, a common vocabulary that allows us to talk about how to craft prose, a useful way to explain and categorize the word patterns we call sentences. Learning these terms is not the goal. The goal, as always, is good writing—putting words together with precision and pizzazz. Should you find yourself caught up in the categories or puzzling over the patterns, remember that when we investigate the sentence, we are investigating a familiar subject, an old friend.

On, then, to the sentence. A *sentence* is a self-contained grammatical unit that ends with a full-stop punctuation mark (period, question mark or exclamation mark—but please, please, take it easy on the exclamation points!) A sentence must contain a verb and a subject (stated or implied), and it must state a complete thought.

A sentence can be as concise as a single word: *Go. Stop. Wait.* (The subject, *you*, is implied.) It can be as expansive (and exhausting) as the 4,391-word sentence James Joyce wrote in *Ulysses*. Regardless of length, grammatically correct sentences result from the same procedure: the selection, manipulation and coordination of sentence parts.

Sentence Parts

Predicates and Subjects

A sentence can be divided into two parts: the *predicate* and the *subject*. The *simple predicate* of a sentence is the verb. The *simple subject* is the noun or noun substitute that identifies the "actor" or initiator of action in a sentence, as in:

The telemarketer   called.
(simple subj.)   (simple pred.)

The *complete predicate* includes the verb plus all its complements and modifiers—words, phrases or clauses that add specificity and meaning. The *complete subject* includes the noun or noun substitute and all its complements and modifiers:

The fast-talking telemarketer   **called at dinner time.**
(complete subj.)   (complete pred.)

We can continue to describe and modify both the subject and the predicate parts of the sentence:

The insistent, fast-talking telemarketer   **always called at dinner time.**
(complete subj.)   (complete pred.)

In addition to modifiers and descriptive phrases, action verbs can be complemented by direct objects, indirect objects and prepositional phrases—all of which are considered part of the predicate. A *direct object* is any noun or pronoun that answers the question *what?* or *whom?* An *indirect object* tells *to whom* or *for what* that action is done. A *prepositional phrase* is a preposition followed by its object. These complements must be in the objective case. Recognizing them will help you avoid making errors in case:

The telemarketer was selling   <u>**gym memberships.**</u>
                                          (noun as dir. obj.)

I gave the <u>telemarketer</u>   **ten <u>seconds</u> of my time.**
      (noun as indir. obj.)   (noun as dir. obj.)

I responded   <u>**with profanity.**</u>
                         (prep. phrase)

I responded to   <u>**him**</u>.
                            (pron. as obj. of prep., in objec. case)

The complement of a linking verb is a noun or an adjective describing the subject. These words are also considered part of the predicate:

The telemarketer was a   <u>**jerk.**</u>
                                    (pred. nom.)

I was   <u>**annoyed**</u>.
                   (pred. adj.)

Phrases and Clauses

Phrases and clauses are the building blocks of sentences. A *phrase* is a group of related words that lacks a verb. Phrases come in two basic varieties: a *prepositional phrase* (a preposition followed by its object) and a *verbal phrase* (a form of the verb—infinitive, gerund or participle—that *does not act as a verb*, accompanied by its object or related material). Verbals are also discussed on p. 46.

During dinner every night that week, another telemarketer called.
(prep. phrase)

My one wish was   **to enjoy an uninterrupted meal.**
                           (infin. phrase, acting as a pred. noun)

Turning off the phone was the obvious solution.
(gerund phrase, acting as a noun ... substitute "it" for the phrase)

Grabbing the phone with one hand, I stirred the spaghetti with the other.
(pres. participial phrase, acting as adj. modifying *I*)

Distracted by the noodles, I dropped the phone in the pot
(past participial phrase, acting as adj. modifying *I*)
of boiling water.

Recognizing phrases and knowing what functions they perform can help you build interesting sentences that not only say what you want them to say but say what you want them to say crisply, clearly and with style. Understanding phrases can also help you avoid at least two common errors in writing: fragments and dangling participle phrases. If you know that a phrase, however lengthy or complex, is not a sentence, then you will not mistake it for one, punctuate it as one and, in the process, create an ungrammatical fragment. If you understand what a participle phrase is and recognize that its purpose is to modify a noun, then you know the noun must be evident, and the phrase must be placed as close as possible to that noun.

A *clause* is a group of related words that contains a subject and a predicate. An *independent* or *main clause* is a complete sentence:

My housemate   **laughed** hysterically.
(subj.)   (pred.)

A *dependent* or *subordinate clause*, although it also contains a subject and a predicate, does not express a complete thought. It is not a sentence and cannot stand alone:

When she saw my phone slip into the noodle pot
(dependent clause)

When she saw my phone slip into the noodle pot, my housemate
(dependent clause) linked with   (main clause)
laughed hysterically.

Dependent clauses come in three varieties, according to the function they perform in a sentence. A *noun clause* takes the place of a noun or a noun substitute; an *adjective clause* serves as an adjective; an *adverb clause* acts as an adverb.

That I was enraged did not surprise her.
(noun clause acting as the subj.)
(*It*, a pronoun, can be substituted for the clause.)

The telemarkers, **who had mysteriously managed to get my cell phone number and had interrupted dinner every night for a week,**
(adj. clause, modifies the noun *telemarketers*)
had obviously gotten on my nerves.

After I took a deep breath and ate a pint of Cherry Garcia ice cream,
(adv. clause modifies the verb by answering *when?*)
I regained my composure.

Note how subordinating an idea (that is, constructing a subordinate clause for the ice-cream eating frenzy) emphasizes the main idea (the act of regaining composure expressed in the main clause). When you recognize the variety and the many uses of dependent clauses, you enhance your ability to craft great prose.

Types of Sentences

Sentences come in four varieties, depending on the number and type of clauses they contain. Learn—and revel in—this variety. It will add spark and interest to your prose and help you write with both grace and rhythm.

Simple Sentences

A *simple sentence* contains one independent clause. The most common construction is subject–verb–object.

Reporters	interview	sources.
(subj.)	(verb)	(obj.)

We can add modifiers—single words or phrases or a combination of both—but regardless of the number of words, the sentence remains simple if it contains a single, independent clause:

Thoughtful   reporters   intelligently interview   informed   sources
(adj.)   (adv.)   (adj.)
during the course of research.
(prep. phrase)

Note that a simple sentence can have multiple subjects and/or verbs. What keeps the sentence simple is that is contains only one independent clause.

<u>**Reporters and their editors**</u>   <u>**check and recheck**</u> **facts.**
(multiple subj.)   (multiple verb)

Compound Sentences

A *compound sentence* has two or more independent clauses, each containing a subject and a predicate and each expressing a complete thought. The two complete clauses, equal or nearly equal in importance, are linked (coordinated) by a conjunction and a comma, semicolon or colon. *And, but, or, nor* and *yet* are the conjunctions, sometimes referred to as *coordinating conjunctions*:

<u>**The 24/7 news cycle is a reality,**</u> **but** <u>**that doesn't mean reporters and**</u>
(indep. clause)   (conj.)   (indep. clause)
<u>**editors should rush to publish before verifying the facts.**</u>

<u>**Readers expect accuracy;**</u> <u>**reporters must deliver or lose credibility.**</u>
(indep. clauses linked by semicolon)

<u>**Citizen journalists have an important place in world,**</u> **but** <u>**one thing is**</u>
<u>**clear**</u>: <u>**They will never replace professional reporters.**</u>
(three indep. clauses, linked by comma and conj., and colon)

Punctuation is probably the most common problem associated with compound sentences. Because the two (or more) clauses are independent— actually complete sentences on their own—they cannot be linked by a comma or a conjunction alone. A compound sentence needs both a comma and a coordinating conjunction. If you do not want to use a coordinating conjunction, use a semicolon or, occasionally, a colon. We'll focus on punctuation in Chapter 7.

Complex Sentences

A *complex sentence* contains one independent (main) clause and at least one dependent (subordinate) clause. The subordinate clause depends on the main clause for both meaning and grammatical completion:

<u>**Before she saw the documentary *Food, Inc.*,**</u>   <u>**she had never**</u>
(dep. clause)   (indep. clause)
<u>**considered raising her own chickens.**</u>

<u>**A backyard coop is easy to maintain,**</u>   <u>**although it is not a**</u>
(indep. clause)   (depend. clause)
<u>**pleasant chore.**</u>

In the two preceding complex sentences, conjunctions (*before, although*) introduce the dependent clauses. These words, sometimes called *subordinating conjunctions*, establish the relationship between the two sentence parts. Our language has a variety of such words, each with its own precise meaning that expresses a specific relationship between the dependent and the independent clauses. For example:

Relationship	Conjunctions
cause and effect	because, due to, as a result of, if
sequence	after, before, during, while
time, place	when, whenever, since, where, until, as long as

A dependent clause can also be subordinated to the main clause by relative pronouns (*who, whom, whose, which* or *that*). Note that the main clause can be interrupted by the dependent clause:

The farmer   **who sold us the baby chicks**   **assured us they**
(dep. clause)
were all female.

Compound–Complex Sentences

A *compound–complex* sentence contains at least two main clauses and one dependent clause. The construction seems to invite wordiness, but it also makes rhythm and flow possible if you are careful, precise and grammatical. Here is a four-clause sentence that works:

After the chicks were three months old,
(dep. clause)

the Golden-laced Wyondotte started crowing,
(indep. clause)

and   **we realized the sad truth:**
(indep. clause)

We had a non-egg-laying rooster on our hands.
(indep. clause)

If you find that a compound–complex sentence is out of control— so complicated that readers will lose the thread, so long that broadcasters will gasp for breath—break the sentence into two (or more) parts, being careful to maintain the relationship between subordinate and main thoughts.

> ### A good sentence
>
> It's craft, but it's also art. It's hard, purposeful work, but there's a bit of alchemy to it. You begin by choosing words, respectful of their meanings, aware of their sounds and rhythms. You fit the words together, carefully, precisely, creatively, to build phrases and clauses. These you link with just the right word, the correct piece of punctuation. You rework, edit, revise.
>
> Then you read what you have written. It says precisely what you want it to say. It has grammatical unity. The idea is coherent; the statement, concise; the language, powerful. You sit back to marvel.
>
> You have written a good sentence.

Sentence Errors

Don't fall prey to one of the following ungrammatical or sluggish constructions: sentence fragment, run-on sentence, over-subordination, dead construction, passive voice. But if you do, don't panic. You can catch this at the editing stage if you know what to look for.

Sentence Fragments

Because fragments are common in casual communication, from tweets to texts, to emails, to blog posts, and because they are so often employed in advertising copy, it's easy to forget that fragments are, in fact, ungrammatical. A *fragment*, literally an incomplete piece, is a group of words sheared off from or never attached to a sentence. The group of words may lack a subject, a predicate, a complete thought or any combination of the three. No matter what it lacks, it is not a grammatical sentence. If you punctuate it as if it were a sentence, you have created a fragment.

Like this one.

Fragments can be single words, brief phrases or lengthy dependent clauses. The number of words is irrelevant. What matters is that the words do not meet the definition of a sentence. A common mistake is to look only for subject and verb and, having found them, to believe that you have written a complete sentence. Remember, a sentence must express a complete thought.

Although the video went viral.
contains a subject (*video*) and a verb (*went*) but does not express a complete thought. It is a dependent clause, a fragment.

Avoiding or rewriting fragments is not difficult. First, recognize that the word, phrase or clause you've written does not meet the definition of a sentence. Now you have two choices: (1) Rewrite this fragment to include all the parts it needs (subject, verb, complete thought); or (2) add to the fragment, making it a complete sentence. Here's how it works:

Although the video went viral.
(fragment)

The video went viral.
(fragment rewritten as a complete thought)

Although the video went viral, Hollywood agents still did not call.
(fragment now part of a complete thought)

Some accomplished writers will tell you that fragments serve a useful purpose. We agree. In appropriate instances, to achieve particular effects, certain grammatical rules can be broken—and this is one of them. *Purposeful fragments*—consistent with the subject, the audience and the medium—are a matter of style. *Accidental fragments* are a grammatical error. Put another way: To break the rule, you have to know the rule.

Run-On Sentences

A *run-on sentence* doesn't know when to quit. Rushing forward without proper punctuation, this construction may actually include two or three complete sentences. Length is not the issue here. A relatively short sentence, like this one, can be a run-on:

Her blog attracted thousands of visitors a day, she was offered a lucrative book deal.

This sentence is actually two independent clauses run together with a comma. Using commas to link independent clauses (without the help of a conjunction) almost always results in a run-on sentence. In fact, this comma-splice error is the most common cause of run-on sentences. But if you can recognize an independent clause, and if you understand the limitations of the comma, you can avoid the error.

The most frequently used of all punctuation marks, the comma serves a variety of purposes. But one job a comma rarely performs is linking independent clauses. This function is performed by the semicolon or, occasionally, the colon. When you force the comma to do a job for which it was not designed, you create a grammatically incorrect construction.

Occasionally—and knowingly—a writer might violate the comma-splice rule. When a sentence is composed of two or more brief, parallel clauses, commas might be used:

Be correct, be concise, be coherent.

Comma-splice run-ons, in addition to being grammatically incorrect, almost always lack clarity. A comma signals readers that they are reading one continuous idea interrupted by a brief pause (the comma). Readers expect the words following the comma to augment or complement what they have just read. But in a comma-splice run-on, there is not one continuous idea. New thoughts are introduced without the benefit of connections between them (for example, *but, and* or *or*).

You can easily correct a run-on sentence in four ways:

1. Change the run-on sentence to two (or more) complete sentences by adding periods and capital letters:

   Her blog attracted thousands of visitors a day. She was offered a lucrative book deal.

2. If the relationship between the two (or more) complete thoughts (clauses) is close and equal, insert a semicolon between them to express this. A semicolon shows this connection and allows the reader to move swiftly from the first sentence to the second. But semicolons are somewhat formal and a little stodgy. They may not work in all instances:

   Her blog attracted thousands of visitors a day; she was offered a lucrative book deal.

3. If the two thoughts are of equal weight and have a connection that can be signaled by a coordinating conjunction (*and, but, or, nor, yet* or *so*), use a comma and the appropriate conjunction to link the clauses:

   Her blog attracted thousands of visitors a day, so she was offered a lucrative book deal.

4. If the relationship between the two (or more) independent clauses is such that one clause depends on the other, rewrite the "dependent" sentence as a clause and place it in front of or after the main clause. Choose a subordinating conjunction that expresses the nature of the relationship, and place it appropriately. Subordinating conjunctions include *after, because, while, when, where, since, if* and *although*.

   Because her blog attracted thousands of visitors a day, she was offered a lucrative book deal.

Over-subordinated Sentences

Subordination, the fourth way just listed to correct a run-on sentence, is the technique of making one idea less important than, or subordinate to, another. Consider these sentences:

Lizzie Hager won the $200-million Powerball jackpot.

Lizzie Hager purchased only a single Powerball ticket.

Assuming the idea in the first sentence is the more important one, you can subordinate the idea in the second sentence by creating a dependent clause and attaching it to the main clause.

Although Lizzie Hager purchased only a single ticket,
(subordinate clause)

she won the $200-million Powerball jackpot.

Lizzie Hager, who had purchased only a single ticket, won the
(subordinate clause)
$200-million

Powerball jackpot.

Subordinating one idea to another is a useful sentence-building technique. But do take care. A string of dependent clauses, or one excessively long dependent clause, placed before the main sentence can slow the pace. You make your readers or listeners wait too long to get to the important idea, and you risk losing and confusing them.

After losing her job and having her car repossessed, although she was not a risk-taker and despite the fact that she purchased only a single ticket, Lizzie Hager won the $200-million Powerball jackpot.
(over-subordination)

There are too many ideas here for one sentence. The three subordinate clauses that precede the main idea bog down the sentence and slow the reader's comprehension. The sentence needs to be rewritten, shortening and combining the introductory ideas or giving them a sentence of their own. Note that over-subordination can happen at the end of the sentence too, with the main clause coming first, and a do-not-know-when-to-quit string of dependent clauses tacked on at the end. A sloppy writer can also over-subordinate by sandwiching the main clause between two (or more) dependent clauses. These over-subordinated sentences may not be certifiably awful, but they are certainly not graceful—or reader-friendly.

Dead Constructions

Perhaps they are holdovers from term paper writing style, but these constructions have a limited place in good writing: *it is* and *there is*. In most cases these words merely take up space, performing no function in the sentence. They not only add clutter but also often rob the sentence of its power by shifting emphasis from what could be a strong verb to a weaker construction—a linking verb (*is, was* and other forms of *to be*):

There was a   **<u>flood</u> downtown.**
                       (verb potential)

Downtown   **<u>flooded.</u>**
                       (stronger verb)

In addition to strengthening the sentence by using an action verb, avoiding *there is/there are* constructions has another benefit: simpler subject—verb agreement. (See our discussion of *There is/There are* as "false subjects" in Chapter 6.) *There* is not usually a subject. Whether you use *is* or *are* depends on what follows the verb:

There <u>is</u> a <u>sale</u> on smartphones.
       (subj.)

There <u>are</u> special <u>discounts</u> for students.
               (subj.)

Looking for the subject after the verb can create agreement confusion. Avoid both the confusion and the dead construction by restructuring the sentence. For example:

Smartphones are on sale. Students are eligible for special discounts.

It is/there is constructions are not entirely without value. You might purposefully choose this structure to create a particular rhythm and emphasis as in this memorable construction, the opening of Charles Dickens' *A Tale of Two Cities*:

It was the best of times, it was the worst of times; it was the age of wisdom, it was the age of foolishness; it was the epoch of belief, it was the epoch of incredulity; it was the season of Light, it was the season of Darkness; it was the spring of hope, it was the winter of despair …

A good rule to follow is this: If *it is/there is* merely takes up space in the sentence, restructure the sentence. Rescue the "hidden verb" and avoid agreement problems. If on occasion you want to emphasize the subject—or have fun parodying Dickens—use *it is/there is*—but sparingly.

Passive Voice

Awkwardness is caused when passive voice is used. Power is robbed from sentences, and stiltedness is caused. Strong verbs are weakened.

> **When writers use passive voice, they create awkward prose and powerless, stilted sentences with weakened verbs.**

Read the first example again. Does the language sound clumsy and unnatural, lifeless and detached? We think so. This is passive-voice construction at work. Now read the second example, with the ideas rewritten in the active voice. If you can recognize the improvement—the leaner construction, the faster pace, the straightforward design, the strong, unencumbered verbs—you know why active voice is *almost always* preferable. We'll talk more about passive voice in our chapter on clarity and conciseness. Here, let's review what passive voice is and set you on a path that (mostly) avoids such deadening sentence construction.

What is passive voice?

Voice refers to the form of the verb. The subject acts when you use the *active voice* verb form. In the *passive voice*, the person or thing performing the action becomes instead the object of the sentence; it does not act, but is acted *upon* by the verb:

He photographed the homeless teens.
(active)

The homeless teens were photographed by him.
(passive)

Photographs were taken of the homeless teens.
(passive)

In the first sentence, the actor (*He*) is performing the action (*photographed*) on the recipient of the action (*the homeless teens*). In the second sentence, the recipients (*teens*) are having the action (*photographed*) performed on them by the actor (*him*). The second sentence is an awkward inversion of the first. Look at it this way:

Active Construction

who	did what	to whom
actor	performed action	on recipient
He	photographed	teens

Passive Construction

who	had what done to it	by whom
recipient	acted upon	by actor
teens	were photographed	by him

The third sentence is also in the passive voice. Here the actor—*who* took the photographs—is missing. The recipient (*teens*) is being acted upon (*photographed*), but we do not know by whom.

Unless something else is structurally wrong with a passive-voice sentence, it is not technically a grammatical error. In fact, all three of the examples above are grammatically correct. But the first sentence is lean and straightforward, and the second is clumsy and stilted. The third does not do the job we expect of a good sentence. It does not tell us all the information.

Keep in mind that although passive-voice construction does use *to be* verb forms, many *to be* forms are in the active voice.

She was posting status updates four times a day.
(active)

Here the actor (*she*) performs the action (*posting*). The order is straightforward: Who did what. The *was* does not signal passive voice; it is merely a *helping* or *auxiliary* verb. For this sentence to be in the passive voice, it would have to be constructed like this:

Status updates were being posted by her four times a day.
(passive)

Note that *status updates*, the recipient of the action, is now the subject of the sentence. The actor, *she*, who was the subject of the first sentence, now appears as the object. The order is inverted; the result is clumsy.

Don't try to identify passive voice by the tense of the verb or by the presence of auxiliary verbs. Instead, find the verb and ask: Who or what is performing this action? If the actor (the *who*) is missing, or if the actor is having the action performed on it rather than directly doing the action, the sentence is passive.

Take another look at one of the sentences from the beginning of this section:

Awkwardness is caused when passive voice is used.
(Who/what causes awkwardness? Who uses passive voice?)

When writers use passive voice, they create awkward prose.
(Active voice: who does what to whom)

Remember: Although passive voice is not grammatically incorrect, it is a roadblock on the path to good, strong writing. Why?

Passive voice tends to dilute the verb of its power because the relationship between action and actor is indirect rather than straightforward:
The rebels were surrounded by the militia. (passive)

The militia surrounded the rebels.
(active)

Passive voice can also bury the verb just as there is/there are constructions do. Look at what happens to the strong, direct verb *accused* in the following sentences:

The committee accused the athlete of doping.
(active)

Accusations were made by the committee about the athlete's alleged doping.
(passive)

The passive-voice sentence changes the verb *accused* to the noun *accusations*. The result is a flabby sentence.

Passive voice may intentionally or accidentally obscure who or what is responsible for an action by omitting the identity of the actor from the audience:

Mistakes were made.

Who made these mistakes? The passive-voice construction masks the identity of the responsible entity, but who or what is responsible for an action may be vital information. It may be the *most* vital information! Consider the vastly different implications of the following sentences:

"Mistakes were made," the president said at the morning press conference.

"I made mistakes," the president admitted at the morning press conference.

The inclusion of the *who* makes quite a difference. We'll discuss other clarity-related reason to avoid passive voice in Chapter 8.

Correcting passive voice

Unless you have a specific reason to use passive voice (see p. 36), avoid it by constructing or rewriting sentences in the active voice. Remember: In the active voice, the actor performs the action. That doesn't mean that all sentences will be alike. You can vary sentences by placement of phrases and clauses, by length, by internal rhythm, by any number of stylistic decisions.

Correcting passive voice is simple once you recognize the construction. Here's how:

1. Find the verb in the sentence.

2. Ask yourself *who* or *what* is performing the action of the verb. When you do this, you are identifying the actor in the sentence. Keep in mind that

some passive-voice sentences omit the real actor (as in the *Mistakes were made* example.) You may not be able to find the person or thing responsible for the action in the sentence; you may have to add it.

3. Construct the sentence so that the real actor performs the action.

Now let's go through the three steps, beginning with the following passive-voice sentence:

An exposé of the doping scandal is being written by the young reporter.

1. The verb is *is being written.*

2. *Who* performed the action? *Who* is writing? *The reporter.* He or she should be the subject of the sentence.

3. Construct the sentence so that the actor performs the action:

The young reporter is writing an exposé of the doping scandal.

When passive voice is justified

Because passive-voice construction reverses the order of a sentence from actor–verb–recipient to recipient–verb–actor, it can be a useful and justifiable construction when (1) the recipient is more important than the actor, or (2) the actor is unknown, irrelevant or impossible to identify.

In certain instances, the recipient of the action is more important (in journalism, more *newsworthy*) than the performer of the action:

The athlete was ousted from the team by the investigating committee.

The verb is *ousted. Who* ousted? The investigating committee. But clearly the object of the indictment—the athlete—takes precedence in the sentence. It is the newsworthy element. Passive voice is justified here.

The athlete and his trainer were arrested this morning after a raid at a local gym.

The verb is *arrested. Who* arrested? The sentence does not tell us. The person or persons performing the action in the sentence are missing. But because arrests are almost always made by law enforcement personnel, the actor is far less important than the recipients of the action—the athlete and his trainer. Passive voice is allowable, even preferable, in this example as well.

Sometimes the *who* or *what* performing the action is unknown or difficult to identify. When the doer cannot be identified, the writer has little choice but to construct a passive-voice sentence. In this case passive voice is appropriate:

The pharmacy was burglarized sometime late last night.

The verb is *burglarized. Who* or *what* burglarized the pharmacy? The desperate athlete? His misguided trainer? A trio of 10-year-old girls? The doer of this action is unknown. The recipient of the action—the object of the burglary—assumes the prominent place in the sentence.

Shifting voices

Here's an easy rule: Do not change voice from active to passive, or vice versa, within a sentence. This muddled construction shifts focus and confuses the audience. Active voice emphasizes the doer. Passive voice emphasizes the recipient:

The team manager expressed concern over the doping scandal, but the athlete's arrest was not mentioned in his press conference today.

The focus of the first part of the sentence is *the team manager*, the doer or actor. The focus of the second part of the sentence is *the athlete's arrest* (the recipient of the action), resulting in a confusing and awkward shift that adds unnecessary words and robs the second verb, *mentioned*, of its power. (This sentence also lacks parallel structure, which we discuss in Chapter 6.) The sentence would be stronger and clearer if both parts were in the active voice.

The team manager expressed concern over the doping scandal in yesterday's speech but avoided any mention of the athlete's arrest.

Pay particular attention to shifts to the passive after an impersonal *one* or *you*:

If you exercise aerobically, mental acuity can be improved.

The first part of the sentence is in the active voice. The second part shifts the emphasis from the actor (*you*) to the recipient (*mental acuity*). Keep both sentence parts in the active voice for clarity:

If you exercise aerobically, you can improve your mental acuity.

Better yet:

Aerobic exercise improves mental acuity.

The Lead Sentence

Let's end this discussion of the sentence with a few thoughts about the single most important sentence you will write: the *first* sentence. Capturing someone's attention in our media-saturated environment is a tremendous challenge. The competition for attention is staggering: Social media sites, news sites, 24/7 broadcast (or streamed) news, magazines (online and on paper), even—yes, they still exist—newspapers. There are so many millions of blogs that no one really knows how many million there are. A writer using any of these conduits and hoping to ensnare a reader, listener or viewer will have to do it in one quick, powerful motion: the first sentence.

That sentence can be a simple (but reader-enticing) question, like this one that begins a post at an environmental blog:

Are you sick of being awash in greenwashing?

It can be a bold, provocative sentence, like this one that introduces an eight-page advertising insert for the famous M.D. Anderson Cancer Center at the University of Texas:

Everything causes cancer.

It can be foreboding, the kind of sentence that compels a reader to keep reading, like this one that began a 5,000-word magazine feature:

Fourteen months ago, Tom McDonald heard the news no one wants to hear.

In a traditional news story (wherever it appears), the first sentence is designed to give the audience a concise, comprehensive summary of the most important elements of the story. With its admonishments to tell everything (who? what? when? where? how?) in one sentence, the summary lead approach can open the door to bad writing. Packing a sentence with all this material increases the chance that you will write an awkward, muddled, rambling or otherwise confusing sentence.

Did you hear that? That was the click of a reader exiting your story, the ruffle of a page being turned. That was an opportunity lost, a person who will not be reading (or listening to) your words because you didn't put sufficient thought, energy and grammatical know-how into your very first sentence.

We don't want that to happen to you. You have the power—the obligation!—to construct all your sentences both grammatically and gracefully. Let's get to it: the most important word in a sentence, the vibrant core, the verb.

....

For additional resources go to **www.cengagebrain.com**

....

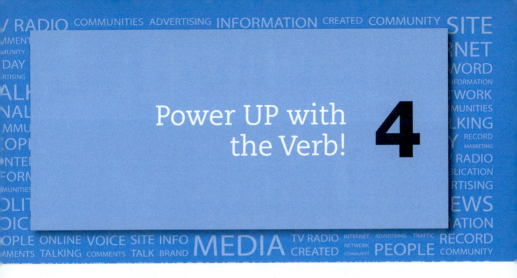

Let's face it: Good writing doesn't come easily.

Talent and style are great allies, but mastering the anatomy of communication also is necessary for your success. In this and several succeeding chapters, we will outline and explain key components of writing, as well as some guidelines to help you avoid errors that will hurt your credibility as a writer.

As we discussed in Chapter 3, the sentence is an assemblage of words that play distinct roles. We call them "parts of speech." Although there are eight of them, one towers above the others: the *verb*.

You can't write a complete sentence without a verb. However, you will write a weaker sentence if you don't employ the strongest, most focused verb.

We must understand verbs in order to construct sentences that give power and precision to our communication. So, we will examine the verb according to forms and functions, number and person, tense, principal parts, voice, and mood. (Sounds like a lot of grammar, yes? *Trust us*—you need to know this!)

We'll conclude this chapter with a discussion of verbals, which may seem to have the power of verbs but in reality are nouns, adjectives or adverbs. *Don't be fooled!*

Verbs Propel Our Sentences

Verb comes from the Latin *verbum*, which means "the word." The verb is at the core of all writing: It is the powertrain of our communication.

A sentence goes nowhere without a verb. At a minimum, a complete sentence must contain a *subject* (a starting point) and a *verb* (providing the power or action), as in

The protestors   **screamed.**
(subj.)   (verb)

However, as you will recall from Chapter 3, the following cannot be a sentence:

The protestors' screams

Why? These three words contain an image but not a complete thought. They need a verb. *Screams* may seem like an action, but it's a label—a *noun*. So, this is not a sentence but a *phrase*—a group of related words that doesn't contain a verb.

Of course, a complete sentence can contain a single word, as in

Wait!
(The subject, the pronoun *you*, is understood)

The verb focuses, directs and commands. Let's examine how the verb functions in its three basic forms. As we do, note the role of a sentence's subject as well as the words that follow the verb.

Verb Forms and Functions

In most writing, a verb states an *action or effort*, which is expressed in *transitive* and *intransitive* verbs.

The blizzard	**struck**	**the city with a fury.**
(subject)	(trans. verb)	(direct object)

Note how *city* receives the action of *struck*. The verb is transitive because the action moves (crosses) directly from the verb to the object of its action.

The blizzard	**slammed into the city without warning.**
(subject)	(intrans. verb)

(The verb is called intransitive because the action does not go directly to an object or recipient. Although this verb has power, it tells us *where* or *how*, but rarely what. We call "into the city" a prepositional phrase.

The third verb form is called *linking*. Consider it a "softer" form of a verb that indicates a *state of being* or a *condition*. These verbs are often a form of *is*:

The blizzard	**is the worst in the city's history.**
(subject)	(linking verb)

The verb is links the subject to a descriptor—*worst*—to reflect a *condition* ("worst blizzard) rather than an action. In all of these examples, the verb directs the sentence.

These verbs are different in how they portray action, show direction or connect a sentence's subject to a description or qualification.

Understanding these forms is key to making correct choices of *case* (discussed in Chapter 6), to preventing the use of an adverb where an adjective belongs, and to avoiding errors with such troublesome verb pairs as *lay/lie* and *sit/set*. There are many more reasons to understand them, as you will discover.

Here's one more look at verb forms, to emphasize differences:

1. **Transitive verb.** In Latin, *trans* means "through" or "across." This verb moves action from the subject to an object, as in:

<u>Helen</u>	<u>wrote</u>	**100 emails in four hours.**
(subj.)	(trans. verb)	(dir. obj.)

   Remember that transitive verbs are always followed by a *direct object—* the recipient of the verb's action. When you can answer the question *what* or *whom* after a verb, you usually have a direct object.

2. **Intransitive verb.** As the prefix *in* suggests, this verb form is not transitive. Although there is no recipient of any action from this type of verb, sentences with intransitive verbs do convey action as well as a sense of location or some description of that action. Here is an example, with *write* in the past tense:

<u>She</u>	<u>wrote</u>	<u>promptly</u> **to the impatient editor.**
(subj.)	(intrans. verb)	(adverb describing the verb)

   Note that in intransitive verb constructions, the words following the verb generally reply to *where, how* or *when.* So, intransitive verbs do *not* take direct objects. These verbs are generally followed by prepositional phrases or adverbs.

3. **Linking verb.** This verb form may seem less forceful compared with its transitive and intransitive cousins, but it has an important role in linking the subject with a descriptor or a concept:

<u>Writing</u>	<u>is</u>	<u>difficult</u> **for her.**
(subj.)	(linking verb)	(pred. adj. describing *writing*)

   Nouns and pronouns can also follow linking verbs. They are called *predicate nominatives*, because they simply restate the subject or connect a related concept to it, as in:

<u>Good writing</u>	<u>is</u>	**her constant <u>goal.</u>**
(subj.)	(linking verb)	(predicate nom.)

   It is usually easy to have the subject switch places with the predicate nominative, to reflect the connection (linkage) between both, as in

Her constant goal is good writing.

The most common verb in these linking constructions is a form of *to be*—as in *is, are, was, were*, and so on. However, there are a number of linking verbs that are not *to be* constructions, although they indicate a state of being. These linking verbs include:

appear	become	feel	get	grow	look
remain	seem	smell	sound	taste	turn

Verb Number and Person

The number and person of a verb are key to proper *agreement*—a tenet of grammar we'll examine in some depth in Chapter 6. Here is the basic rule: *The number of the verb (singular or plural) must match the number of the subject of the sentence.* This requires that the writer identify the *true* subject of the sentence. Verbs in several tenses have numbers, to match the subject number. Some examples:

writes (singular)	write (plural)
has written (singular)	have written (plural)
does (singular)	do (plural)
is (singular)	are (plural)
was (singular)	were (plural)

Person is also an important part of agreement. This concept is embedded in our everyday speech and usually comes naturally. Our grammar "employs" six persons—three singular and three plural. Let's use the verb *is* (derived from *to be*) to show how verbs change their forms depending on the person used. We'll use personal pronouns as the subjects.

First person singular pronoun (*I*):

I am a student of great writing.

Second person singular (*you*):

You are a terrific writer.

Third person singular (*he, she, it*):

She is a gifted editor.

or

A good writer <u>is</u> not always a good editor.

First person plural (*we*):

We <u>are</u> dedicated to preserving longform writing.

Second person plural (*you*):

You <u>are</u> the future of good writing.

Third person plural (*they*):

They <u>are</u> going to succeed as writers.

Note the number of the transitive verb *enjoy* in this sentence:

They <u>enjoy</u> great writing.

The verb *enjoy* is plural. Many third-person singular verbs in the present tense end in *s*, as in

She <u>enjoys</u> great writing.

Common subject verb agreement errors

Here is a brief look at some errors we will discuss in Chapter 6. These examples show the *incorrect* verb choice—*choosing a plural verb when a singular one is needed*:

The <u>rate</u> of unemployment claims <u>are dropping</u>.

The noun or pronoun that is closest to the verb is not necessarily the subject of the sentence. The true subject here is *rate*—a singular noun—so the verb should be *is dropping*. Yes, a verb can be more than one word!

The true subject might not precede the verb, either, as in this example:

Among the many reasons for these writing errors <u>are</u> poor proofreading.

The true subject here is the singular noun *proofreading*. The verb should be *is*.

Verb Tense

Verb *tense*, a "time stamp" in a sentence, indicates present, past, future or ongoing activity. (Note that all the sentence examples in the "number and person" section were written in the present tense.) Here are examples of three common tenses, using the *third-person* singular form of *writes*:

He <u>writes</u> frequently to his grandparents. (present tense)
Harold <u>wrote</u> to his state representative about the farm bill. (past tense)
The principal <u>will write</u> her report soon. (future tense)

In addition, we have six other tenses, three in the *perfect* form and three in the *progressive* form. Briefly, here are those forms, showing just the verbs. You'll note that verb combinations (with auxiliaries) are used to create these forms:

has written (present perfect tense)
had written (past perfect tense)
will have written (future perfect tense)

The progressive forms indicate some form of ongoing or continuous action, even if it details some future action:

is writing (present progressive tense)
had been writing (past progressive tense)
will have been writing (future progressive tense)

It is important to keep tenses "in step," or parallel. Changing tenses unnecessarily creates confusion. We examine parallel structure in Chapter 6.

Let's look briefly at some verbs that change more than most typical or *regular* ones, as we examine *principal parts*.

Principal Parts of Verbs

Verbs have four principal parts: the *to* (infinitive) form to establish its root (as an indicator of the present) and three tenses—past, past participle and present participle. This terminology is less important than your understanding of how verbs change according to their "time stamp."

Let's focus on the "regular" verb *call*, so labeled because its past tense and past participle form have an - *ed* ending and its present participle has an -*ing* ending.

Tom <u>called</u> the mayor about the police contract.
(past tense)

She <u>has called</u> more than 100 of the theater's donors.
(past participle, creating the present perfect tense)

The protestors <u>are calling</u> for the prime minister's resignation.
(present participle, creating the present progressive tense)

Not all verbs are regular. *Irregular* verbs change their form, depending on their tense. Here is a brief list of frequently used irregular verbs; note how the forms change, sometimes dramatically.

Infinitive	Past Tense	Past Participle	Present Participle
to arise	arose	(has) arisen	(is) arising
to begin	began	begun	beginning
to choose	chose	chosen	choosing
to fly	flew	flown	flying
to lay	laid	laid	laying
to lie	lay	lain	lying
to ring	rang	rung	ringing
to rise	rose	risen	rising
to set	set	set	setting
to sit	sat	sat	sitting
to steal	stole	stolen	stealing
to write	wrote	written	writing

Most dictionaries will show common tenses when you look up the verb. Some don't change at all—look up "burst."

Voice

Chapter 3 discussed the active and passive "voices" of verbs. The active voice is clearer, crisper and more complete.

<u>Kim wrote</u> her law school admissions essay this morning.

The action moves from transitive verb to direct object, from *wrote* to *essay*. In active voice constructions, the subject (Kim) performs the action. Generally this is a more direct and concise form of writing.

In the passive voice, the subject of the sentence is acted upon by the verb:

Her law school admission essay <u>was written</u> this morning.

The writer of the report is not identified. (Shall we assume the writer was Kim?)

In some instances, the subject acted upon may be more important than the initiator of the action, as in this sentence:

<u>The mayor was attacked</u> this morning by an unknown assailant.

In general, however, using the passive voice creates awkward sentences and occasionally a false formality.

The Mood of Verbs

Verbs have moods. They are *indicative* when they convey a fact or question. They are *imperative* when they issue a command of sorts, and they are *subjunctive* when they convey some information that is actually contrary to fact or possibility. Examples:

Six investigative reporters <u>wrote</u> the award-winning series.
(indicative)

<u>Write</u> that on your blog!
(imperative)

If only I <u>were</u> the writer Elmore Leonard was.
(subjunctive)

The subjunctive mood is often used to express a wish. In the last example, note the use of *I were*, which is the tipoff that the statement is not a likely possibility.

Verbals

It may look like a verb, but walking like a duck doesn't make you one! What looks like a verb but doesn't have the "oomph" to power a sentence? It's the confusingly named *verbal*, which is really a noun or adjective (or occasional adverb). The way it is embedded in a phrase often suggests a strength it simply doesn't have. We hope this brief discussion keeps you from giving such words undeserved power.

Verbals are classified as *gerunds, participles* or *infinitives*. They can be the subject of a sentence; they can be a direct object; or they can modify nouns and pronouns to add description—*but they can never act as a verb.*

1. **Gerunds.** These verbals, which always have an *-ing* ending, have the feel of action but serve only as the subject or object in a sentence:

   <u>Reaching</u> for the stars has become his personal metaphor.
   (gerund as subj.)

   Reaching represents an activity, not an action. If you dropped the verb *has become* from the preceding example, you would have a sentence fragment. Note that *Reaching* is the subject of the sentence (as a singular noun), which means that the sentence requires the singular verb is for proper agreement.

   Here's a pair of gerunds that serves as the object of a transitive verb:

   She <u>enjoys</u>   <u>swimming</u> and <u>weightlifting</u>.
   (verb)   (gerunds as direct objects)

   Remember: *Gerunds are always nouns.* They will act in the sentence the same way as nouns (see p. 40). However, because the gerund has an *-ing* ending, it is sometimes confused with another verbal, the participle.

2. **Participles.** These verbals have either an *-ing* or *-ed* ending and are always used as adjectives. As an adjective (see p. 55), the participle generally will modify (give extra meaning to) a noun or a pronoun. Examples:

<u>Writing under the pen name of Currer Bell</u>, Charlotte Brontë gained eventual literary fame with *Jane Eyre.*￼

Writing modifies the proper noun and subject, Charlotte Brontë. The only verb in this sentence is *gained*. If you merely wrote, "Writing under the pen name of Currer Bell," you would have a sentence fragment.

3. **Infinitives.** These are verbals that are formed by *to* plus (in most cases) the *present tense* of a verb. Infinitives generally are easy to identify; their role as a noun, adjective or adverb, however, is not always so easy to determine. Let's look at three examples.

Good <u>writers</u>   <u>want</u>   <u>to write</u> frequently.
(subj.)   (trans. verb)   (infin.)

In this sentence, *to write* is an infinitive acting as a noun, the object of the transitive verb *need*. The object *to write* answers the question *what*. In the next example, an infinitive works as an adjective modifying a noun that functions as a direct object:

<u>Conner</u>   <u>has</u>   <u>three deadlines</u>   <u>to meet.</u>
(subj.)   (trans. verb)   (dir. obj.)   (infin.)

And in a final example, the infinitive is used as an adverb modifying the predicate adjective *eager*:

<u>Jackson</u>   <u>is</u>   eager   <u>to write a prize-winning story.</u>
(subj.)   (l. v.)   (infin.)

These, then, are the verbals. To recap, a verbal is *not* a verb. (You can *walk* [a real verb] like a duck and *talk* [another one] like a duck, but that doesn't mean you are a duck!) Verbals are only nouns, adjectives or adverbs.

If you recognize and use verbs well, you have a powerful tool at your disposal. You are on your way. If you understand that a phrase has no verbs and that clauses do, you are on your way to effective sentence construction. If you know that this one word

Wait!

is not only a verb but also a complete sentence—and if you understand that

Waiting for Godot

has no verb and is just a simple phrase, then be happy. Very happy. (You know that "very happy" is not a sentence, right?)

What is the "right" verb?

A sentence is strong when its verb—its power train—possesses power and precision. Its meaning and impact are clear. We will discuss how the "right" verb improves clarity in Chapter 8. For now, consider these two sentences:

The mayor <u>said</u> he <u>would not accept</u> the city manager's proposal to increase parking meter fees.
(verbs underlined)

The mayor <u>dismissed</u> the city manager's call for increased
          (verb)
parking fees.

Which is the more precise, more concise sentence? Easy answer! Choose the best verb that properly reflects the impact and tone that is most accurate.

For additional resources go to **www.cengagebrain.com**

In Chapter 4, we called the verb a "powertrain," which suggests the sentence is a vehicle. Now let's consider the sentence as a mighty ship. Successful navigation requires not only a powerful (not power-mad) captain but a dependable and resourceful crew as well.

Our crew is a hardy collection of seven parts of speech, all working with the verb. They will serve you well if you understand their roles and urge them to work together.

Let's look at our crew, beginning with the noun.

Nouns

We hope that you've known for a long time that a *noun* can be a person, place or thing—and that it can appear in many parts of a sentence. Here are a few nouns that we'll use in the following examples:

judge
Sara (called a *proper noun*)
unemployment
bravery
committee's (*possessive* form)

Nouns are not action words, although they can be the initiators or receivers of some action from a verb. Because a noun is such a common component of a sentence, it has many roles.

1. As the *subject* of a sentence:

The <u>judge</u> rejected the defendant's plea bargain.

2. As the *direct object* of a transitive verb:

   The governor named <u>Sara</u> to the budget committee.

3. As the *predicate nominative* of a linking verb:

   Our biggest challenge today is <u>unemployment</u>.

4. As the *object of a preposition*:

   Your speech on <u>bravery</u> was inspiring.

5. As a *possessive* or *modifier* of another noun:

   The dean has rejected the <u>committee's</u> recommendation.

Recognizing and properly using nouns will help you to make correct decisions about agreement and case (Chapter 6).

Pronouns

The pronoun is sometimes called a *noun substitute* because it serves as a "stand-in" for a previously mentioned noun. Properly used, a pronoun adds flexibility and variety to a sentence.

Pronouns can be more challenging to use than nouns, however. Some of the most common grammatical problems related to the use of pronouns in such areas as antecedent agreement, case and selecting the correct pronoun to introduce a dependent clause. (We'll discuss these in Chapter 6.)

First, let's review these pronoun types: *personal, indefinite, relative, interrogative* and *demonstrative*. Identifying and using them well will help you write with more focus and rhythm.

Types of Pronouns

1. **Personal pronoun.** The most common pronoun type, the personal pronoun takes distinct forms in three cases: nominative (subjective), objective and possessive. To show you how different each pronoun is in its three cases, we'll review each one, from *first-person singular* to *third-person plural*.

Nominative	Objective	Possessive
I	me	my/mine
you	you	your/yours
he	him	his
she	her	her/hers

it	it	its
we	us	our/ours
you	you	your/yours
they	them	their/theirs

Because personal pronouns change form, depending on their sentence function, it is important to be aware of these roles. Here are three proper uses of *we*, which is a first-person plural pronoun:

<u>We</u> are eager to read your report.
(*We* is the subject—nominative case.)

Please send this report to <u>us</u> tomorrow.
(*Us* is the object of the preposition *to*—objective case.)

<u>Our</u> presentation won first place.
(*Our* modifies *presentation*—possessive case.)

An important note about its and it's

The personal possessive pronoun often lures an unnecessary apostrophe from the unwary writer. The most common problem is the confusion between *its* and *it's*, which, of course, sound alike. Sadly, this type of error—which is mortifying if it makes it to publication—seems to be cropping up more frequently:

WRONG: The stock market has reached <u>it's</u> highest point in the last 10 years.
(Remember, *it's* means *it is*. Personal pronouns in the possessive case do not require apostrophes.)

This is correct usage for *it's* and *its*:

<u>It's</u> just a matter of time before the stock market hits <u>its</u> all-time high.

Whereas *it's* and *your's* are often used incorrectly as pronouns (and, by the way, there is no such word as *your's*), noun possessives *do* use an apostrophe, as in:

<u>Taylor Swift's</u> latest album
(proper noun)

the <u>public's</u> right to know
(common noun)

2. **Indefinite pronoun.** Pronouns such as *anyone, enough, many, most, none* and *several* reveal little if anything about their gender or number. As such they can cause troublesome subject–verb and antecedent agreement problems. It's important to understand the sense of the sentence so you can properly match subject, verb and *antecedent* (a previous word to which a pronoun refers).

The good news is that only a handful of indefinite pronouns can take either a singular or a plural verb, depending on the sense of the sentence. If the pronoun refers to a singular unit, the verb will be singular. A plural connotation should be easy to detect. These indefinites include:

all   most   none   some

All of the candy <u>has</u> been eaten.

All of the passengers <u>have</u> been rescued.

See our comments in Chapter 6 and in Part Two about *none*, which can be a bit vexing.

Some indefinite pronouns, such as *both, few, many* and *several*, are obviously plural:

Both of these options <u>are</u> risky.

Indefinite pronouns and gender choice. Indefinite pronouns such as *anybody* and *somebody* can hinder correct gender identification, creating awkward writing. So, which of the four choices of personal possessive pronouns is correct?

<u>Anybody</u> can enter <u>his</u> photograph in the competition.
(So, men only?)

<u>Anybody</u> can enter <u>her</u> photograph in the competition.
(Or just women?)

<u>Anybody</u> can enter <u>his or her</u> photograph in the competition.

<u>Anybody</u> can enter <u>their</u> photograph in the competition.

Although the first two choices are exclusionary, the only grammatically incorrect choice is *their; anybody* (any one person) is obviously singular, so you shouldn't connect a plural possessive pronoun to it. However, it is increasingly apparent that the plural choice is the go-to option, especially in informal usage.

Still, we prefer the most inclusive (and grammatically correct) choice: *anybody . . . his or her*. A writer also has the option of using the plural throughout, changing *anybody* to *people*.

3. **Relative and interrogative pronouns.** Pronouns such as *that, which* and *who* are easy to recognize, but they can be difficult to use properly. Note the correct choices (underlined) in the following sentences:

Who/**Whom** did the voters select in the primary?

Susan is the type of executive that/**who** leads by example.

The aircraft carrier Stennis, that/**which** is now heading toward anchorage in Singapore, is an intimidating spectacle.

This is one of those pens **that**/which **writes** under water.

Using these pronouns correctly requires an understanding of antecedent agreement, case and restrictive and nonrestrictive clauses, which we examine in Chapter 6. However, this is an ideal point to cite a common error with relative pronouns—the use of *that* to avoid a *who/whom* selection:

WRONG: The police officers that stopped my car were polite but firm.
(The correct pronoun choice is *who*.)

WRONG: The candidate that the voters elected has been arrested for
(The correct pronoun is *whom*.)
fraud.

Who or *whom*, rather than *that*, must be selected when the antecedent (in these cases, *officers* and *candidate*) is human or has human qualities. In an earlier sentence, the relative pronoun *that* correctly substituted for the noun *pens*.

Note that the relative pronoun *who* has a separate possessive form (remember the *it's/its* issue?). The possessive form of *who* is *whose*—not the subject–verb contraction *who's* (*who is*). Consider this sentence:

Robinson, **whose** candidacy was initially rejected by her party, is a politician **who's** determined to overcome any obstacle.

4. **Demonstrative pronoun.** These pronouns are "pointers"—their focus leaves little room for doubt. They include *this, that, these* and *those*. They can stand alone, as in:

This is your opportunity to excel.
(refers to a specific opportunity)

Adjectives

Properly used, the adjective adds color and dimension to your writing. The *adjective* describes, limits and otherwise qualifies nouns and some pronouns. It cannot modify verbs; that is the realm of the adverb. Adjectives are sometimes called "picture words," but they can be overused and misapplied. Given their many nuances, adjectives challenge the writer to be on target with meaning and intent.

Types of Adjectives

There are two basic types of adjectives: descriptive and limiting.

1. **Descriptive.** The descriptive adjective adds detail and expands images. Consider the differences in these two sentences (adjectives are underlined in the second sentence):

   Rescue workers continued their search for hikers who were feared lost in a cave near the Cathedral National Monument.

   <u>Exhausted</u> rescue workers continued their <u>frantic</u> search for six <u>youthful</u> hikers feared lost in a <u>flooded</u> cave near the Cathedral National Monument.

   The second sentence paints a more detailed and colorful picture, yes?
      Skilled writers use adjectives carefully. They are more concerned with focused content rather than with flashiness. Properly employed, adjectives don't add glitz or fluff; they provide information to create a more complete picture.

2. **Limiting.** The limiting adjective is more spartan and pragmatic than its descriptive relative. Its chief role is to set boundaries and qualify (limit) meaning. Compare the following two examples:

   Hikers lost in the Mount Hood National Forest met their rescuers today after walking out of the wilderness.

   <u>Three</u> elderly hikers lost in the Mount Hood National Forest for <u>three</u> days met their rescuers today after hiking <u>15</u> miles out of the wilderness.

   ("Fifteen miles" carries significant impact, considering the age of the hikers and how long they were lost. Much can be inferred from this, although in this case the writer did not choose to add more descriptive detail, such as *tortuous* or *snow-clogged* miles. The number of hikers and of days they were lost also provide important detail.) More examples:

   "I am responsible for <u>this</u> budget mess," the mayor admitted today.

   (*This*, which can also be a pronoun, becomes an adjective when it modifies a noun, such as *turnover*. Again, the adjective limits [focuses] the meaning of the sentence. The mayor is referring to a specific budget issue.)

   Is there <u>any</u> chance you will change your mind?

(In connecting to the possibility of change, *any* is seen as a limiting adjective because it provides no description or other helpful context. *Each* and *either* also fit into the category of limiting adjectives.)

Degrees of Adjectives

Many adjectives have three forms that show degree, intensity or comparison. For example, the trio of

rich   **richer**   **richest**

moves from the *base* level (*rich*) to a *comparative* level (*richer*) and then to the *superlative* level (*richest*). At the superlative level no higher comparison can be made—that is, it makes no sense (and is ungrammatical) to characterize an individual as "most richest."

Most adjectives take either the *-er* or *-est* suffix to indicate degree. Some adjectives, however, retain their base form and merely add the adverbs *more* and *most* to show a change in degree:

controversial   **more controversial**   **most controversial**

The use of *more* with an adjective in its comparative form, such as *richer*, creates a funny-sounding (and ungrammatical) construction: *more richer*(!). See further discussion of comparatives and superlatives later in the section on adverbs.

The Predicate Adjective

An adjective that follows a linking verb is called a *predicate adjective*. It modifies the subject, which can be either a noun or a pronoun:

These <u>smoke detectors</u> **are** <u>defective</u>.
   (subj.)   (pred. adj.)

Defective is a predicate adjective. The verb *are* links the quality of being defective to the noun *smoke detectors*—thus creating the meaning of *defective smoke detectors*, with the adjective modifying the noun.

Adjectives as Verbals

Two verbals, the participle and the infinitive (see p. 47), can be classified as adjectives. Whereas the participle is always an adjective, the infinitive is an adjective only when it modifies a noun. An infinitive can also act as a noun or an adverb, depending on its role in a sentence.

<u>**Climbing**</u> **over the barbed wire fence, the robber tore his pants.**
(*Climbing*, a participle, modifies the noun *robber*.)

A quick note about the dangling modifier: An often-humorous error occurs with the misplacement of a noun and its participle (modifier), as in this sentence:

Climbing over the barbed wire fence, the robber's pants tore.

As you can see, the pants didn't do the climbing! This is what we call a *dangling* or *misplaced modifier*.

Here is an example of an infinitive that acts as an adjective:

The senator announced her decision <u>to vote</u> against the budget bill.

The infinitive *to vote* modifies the noun *decision*; *to vote* characterizes or helps describe *decision*.

Adverbs

Adverbs can also describe and limit, but in many ways, they have a greater range than adjectives. Here is the "workload" of the adverb:

- Modify a verb

   Paramedics drove <u>carefully</u> through the blast site.
   The adverb *carefully* describes or modifies the verb *drove*; in this type of construction, an adverb often answers the question *how*.

- Modifying an adjective

   This latte is <u>dangerously</u> hot.
   Dangerously modifies the predicate adjective *hot*; pardon the pun, but it states a degree.

- Modifying another adverb

   These new internet stocks performed <u>very</u> badly last quarter.
   Very modifies the adverb *badly* and together they modify the verb *performed*; again, these adverbs answer the question *how*.

- Introducing a sentence

   <u>Why</u> are you bugging me about this?
   Why is an interrogative adverb; it modifies the verb *are bugging*.

- Connect two clauses

   I don't agree with your conclusions; <u>however</u>, I admire the passion of your argument.
   Because it links two clauses that could stand alone as two sentences, *however* is called a *conjunctive adverb*.

Many adverbs end in *-ly*, but don't always count on that for proper identification. Examine a sentence carefully to be sure. For example, *slow* can be both an adjective and an adverb, depending on how it is used in a sentence, but *slowly* can be only an adverb.

As you can see, an adverb can provide the how, where, when and why of a sentence, which shows its close connection to the verb.

Comparatives and Superlatives of Adverbs

An adverb can indicate a comparison between two units; it can also express the highest degree of quality among three or more units.

Here's an example of the adverbial *comparative*, with the sufix *-er*:

Ohio's unemployment rate has risen <u>faster</u> than Indiana's.
(*Comparative*: Two unemployment rates are being compared.)

Here is an example of the *superlative*, with the suffix *-est*:

Ohio's unemployment rate has risen the <u>fastest</u> of all Midwest states.
(*Superlative*: There is no higher degree of comparison available. Put another way, nothing is faster than fastest!)

Remember that not all adverbs use the *-er* and *-est* suffix. Words such as *fearful* and *dangerous* use extra adverbs such as *more* to indicate the comparative and *most* to show the superlative. Obviously, we don't employ both *most* and the *-est* characterization: It is redundant (and silly) to describe someone as the "most smartest" in the class.

A cautionary note

Be sure that your meaning is clear when you employ a comparative or superlative. Consider these errors:

High blood pressure is <u>more</u> dangerous than any chronic health condition in the world today.

Besides being an amazingly sweeping (and arguable) statement, this sentence implies that high blood pressure is also more pernicious than itself, because it, too, is a chronic disease. The last part of the sentence should read *than any **other** chronic health condition in the world today.*

This is the <u>most</u> unique piece of art I have ever seen.

Certain words, called *absolutes*, defy comparisons. *Unique*, an absolute, is already a superlative. So are *perfect, excellent, impossible, final* and *supreme*. This says it all:

This is a <u>unique</u> piece of art.

There's more on this issue in the context of clarity and conciseness in Chapter 8.

Prepositions

Prepositions are both navigators and locators. They connect nouns and pronouns to create phrases, linking these phrases to the rest of a sentence, as in these two examples:

Former Mayor Thompson must report <u>to</u> the Vandalia Prison <u>in</u> two weeks.

and

Your kind words mean a lot <u>to</u> Jane and me.

Like many other parts of speech, prepositions can have tightly focused meanings. Writers sometimes make the wrong choices with such prepositional pairs as *among/between, beside/besides, beneath/below, because of/due to* and *on/upon*. Part Two of this book discusses the differences between these pairs.

The prepositions we most frequently use in our writing include:

about   at   by   down   for   from   in   of   on   to   up   with

Here is a partial list of other prepositions. Note that some are more than one word, whereas others such as *but, like* and *since* can serve as another part of speech, depending on the sense of the sentence.

above	at	except
according to	atop	in back of
across	because of	in front of
after	before	in lieu of
against	behind	in place of
ahead of	below	in spite of
alongside	beneath	instead of
along with	beside	into
amid	besides	in view of
among	between	like
apart from	beyond	near
around	but	nearby
aside from	despite	next to
as of	during	off

on top of	through	with
out	throughout	within
out of	till	without
outside	toward	
owing to	under	
over	underneath	
past	until	
per	unto	
prior to	up	
since	upon	

Prepositions and pronoun case

Although we will examine the principle of case in Chapter 6, this section on prepositions provides a perfect opportunity for case preview. Here is the basic rule: A pronoun *must* be in the objective case when it is the object of the preposition. So, it would *not be correct* to write (or say):

This is a perfect opportunity <u>for you and I.</u>

The personal pronoun *I* changes to *me* in the objective case; the sentence should end with:

. . . for you and <u>me</u>.

The same is true for such phrases as:

according to **<u>her</u>**   for **<u>us</u>**   with **<u>them</u>**

A related note: Just because a prepositional phrase begins a sentence doesn't mean that its object belongs in the nominative (also called subjective) case. "Object" suggests objective case, right? So, this sentence is *incorrect*:

<u>Between you and I,</u> this is going to be an easy test.

And this is correct—always:

<u>Between you and me,</u> I will study harder for this test.

Objects of Prepositions are Not Subjects of a Sentence!

In addition to proper selection of case, writers should also pay attention to subject–verb agreement (which we also discuss in Chapter 6), Consider this sentence:

| **One** | **<u>of these 50-dollar bills</u>** | **<u>is</u> counterfeit.** |
| (subj.) | (prep. phrase) | (l. v.) |

Some writers are tempted to use the plural verb *are*, thinking that the noun *bills* is the subject of the sentence. It's not—*bills* is the object of the preposition *of*; that is the only role *bills* has in this sentence.

A final point about prepositions: What is this business about not ending a sentence with a preposition? If it was good enough for the writer of the hit song "Devil with a Blue Dress On," why can't you end with *with, to* or *on*? We feel the same way about this as we do about cracking open fresh eggs with just one hand: Do it as long as you don't make a mess. Scrambling a sentence to move around a preposition can be awkward:

> **This is a sentence <u>up with which</u> a good writer will not put.**

Strive for clarity rather than rigidity—it will keep you out of trouble.

Conjunctions

Conjunctions are trusty bridges that connect phrases and clauses in a sentence. They help us maintain rhythm and coherence, in addition to creating needed transitions. There are three basic forms of conjunctions; we'll begin with an explanation of conjunctions that coordinate or subordinate; we'll conclude with the correlative conjunction. In Chapter 3, we explained about compound and complex sentences. Remember these sentence types are we move through this discussion.

Coordinating and Subordinating Conjunctions

In its primary role, a conjunction coordinates (balances) clauses and phrases of equal weight. A *coordinating conjunction* can link two independent clauses, which could stand alone as separate sentences:

> **You can't adjust the wind, <u>but</u> you can adjust your sails.**

A coordinating conjunction also links simple words and phrases that show a relationship:

> **Vanessa loves tofu <u>and</u> chocolate.**

> **In a stressful situation, avoid jumping out of the frying pan <u>and</u> into the fire.**

The most common coordinating conjunctions are:

> **and   but   for   nor   or   yet   while**

When conjunctions are used to join clauses of unequal weight (that is, one clause clearly takes precedence and can stand by itself if necessary as a complete sentence), they are called *subordinating conjunctions*. They often are used to introduce some material or to provide context or counterpoint to the main part of the sentence.

In this first example, a subordinating conjunction (underlined) introduces a dependent clause:

<u>Unless</u> management and labor can come to an agreement, the strike will begin at midnight.

The most common subordinating conjunctions are:

after	**although**	**as**	**as if**	**before**	**how**
if	**since**	**so**	**through**	**unless**	**while**

Pay careful attention to use of the subordinating conjunction *as if*. Be wary of substitutes for it; a common error is to use the preposition *like*:

It looks <u>like</u> it will snow today.

Remember that prepositions cannot link a clause—only a phrase or single word. In the previous sentence, a writer has two correct choices:

It looks <u>as if</u> it will snow today.

It looks <u>like</u> snow today.

Correlative Conjunctions

These conjunctions operate in pairs because they join words, phrases and clauses to provide balance:

This class is <u>both</u> challenging <u>and</u> inspiring.

<u>Neither</u> the players <u>nor</u> the coach has met with the media.

(Note: In *either/or* and *neither/nor* constructions, the noun closest to the verb controls the number of the verb, as in *coach has* ...)

The most common correlative conjunctions are:

both ... and	not only ... but also
either ... or	whether ... or
neither ... nor	

Adverbs that look like conjunctions

Words such as *accordingly, consequently, however, moreover, nevertheless* and *therefore* appear to have linking qualities. However, they are adverbs inserted between two independent clauses to provide transition or a change in flow, which is why they also are called *conjunctive adverbs*. Understanding this should help you punctuate correctly.

Our meeting lacks a quorum; <u>therefore</u>, we will adjourn until next Friday.
(Note the use of the semicolon after *quorum*. We discuss this and other punctuation in Chapter 7.)

Interjections: *Bwah-Hah-Hah!*

The *interjection*, a fun and highly inventive part of speech, is often an emotional exclamation. And judging from the heading above, it is a useful ally in social media.

Here are some common interjections:

Ahem Aw Eh Ha Hey Huh Mmm Oh Oops Shh Uh

Among our favorites:

Ew   Feh   Hmph   Ugh   Whew   Yum

An interjection can often stand alone with its own punctuation, as in this sentence fragment:

Wow!

However it is often part of a complete sentence, as in

Whew—this chapter is done!

....
For additional resources go to **www.cengagebrain.com**
....

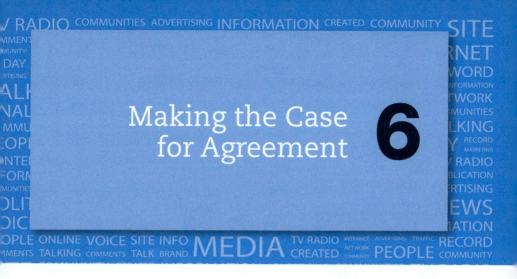

It's not just deadlines and mental blocks that haunt writers. Errors in grammar, usage and spelling also hound them, often with serious consequences.

Consider these thoughts from Corey duBrowa, senior vice president of global communications for Starbucks. With several decades of agency work also in his portfolio, he has high expectations of writing skills.

He says: "Bad writing knows no economic or titular boundary. I look for strong storytelling skills, but I too often see them hampered by problems in grammar, punctuation, *grammar*, vocabulary choices, *grammar*, spelling, *grammar*." He adds that many firms and agencies have programs in mentoring and course "toolkits" to help stamp out poor writing.

In the hope that our point is made, let's examine the key concepts of agreement (subject–verb and subject–antecedent), case and parallel structure. Your thorough understanding of them will prevent a host of regrettable errors and free you to focus on content. Our goal is to bring harmony and balance to your writing.

Subject–Verb Agreement

Master this rule:

- **A verb must agree with the intended <u>number</u> of its subject.**

This requires that you

1. identify the actual subject of the sentence *and*

2. decide the subject's number—singular or plural.

Your understanding of sentence elements (subject, object, etc.) and of parts of speech is critical to your success here. (*Teachable moment*: Did

63

you see that in the previous sentence *understanding*, rather than *elements*, is the sentence's subject?) You know that a subject of a sentence can be either a noun or a pronoun. A subject, of course, is the actor or key starting point of a sentence; it directly connects to the action or state of being of a verb.

Let's recall what a subject is *not*.

- It is *not* the object of a preposition.

   Between <u>these two extremes</u> <u>lies</u> a reasonable <u>solution</u>.
           (obj. of preposition)   (verb)   (subject)

   The real subject is *solution*, a singular noun. *Extremes*, the object of the preposition *between*, is plural; although it is physically close to the verb, *extremes* does not control the verb's number. This example shows that a subject isn't always located at the beginning of a sentence.

- It is not the expletive *there* or *here*.

   <u>There</u> <u>have been</u> many <u>cases</u> of flu reported this week.
   (expl.) (verb)   (subject)

   In this usage, an expletive such as *here* or *there* "anticipates" the subject that follows it. That is why such words are sometimes called *anticipatory subjects*. However, they have no standing as a subject, and in fact their use can be a sign of weak or indirect writing.

- It is not the object of a gerund.

   <u>Running two marathons</u>   <u>is</u>   her goal this year.
   (gerund as subject)   (verb)

   Running, a gerund, is the real subject. As such, *running* is an act, not an action, so it is not a verb; all gerunds are nouns. Remember our discussion on p. 47. *Marathons*, the gerund's object, does not control the verb's number.

- It is not a predicate nominative.

   My biggest <u>concern</u> today   <u>is</u>   <u>health care issues</u>.
         (subject)   (verb—sing.)   (pred. nominative)

   This is an example of how a writer needs to "parse" a sentence to properly connect a subject to its verb. Keep in mind that a predicate nominative, although linked to the subject, does not control the number of the verb. *Concern*, the subject, is singular.

- It is not a phrase that is parenthetical to the true subject.

  Your <u>speech</u>, <u>as well as your volunteer efforts</u>, <u>has impressed</u> the
     (subj.)   (parenthetical phrase)   (verb)
  committee.

  Phrases such as *along with* and *as well as* merely modify the real subject of a sentence. They do not turn that subject into a compound or plural, construction. We have a singular subject and a singular verb.

  Now that we have focused on what a subject is *not*, let's turn to what a subject *is*. Let's examine this area in three ways: (1) when the subject is always singular, (2) when the subject is always plural and (3) when it could be either.

The Always Singular Subject

- As the subject of a sentence, the pronouns *each, either, anyone, everyone, much, one, no one, nothing* and *someone* always take singular verbs.

  <u>Each</u> of these <u>exercise programs</u> has a major flaw.

  Note that *exercise programs*, the object of the preposition *of*, cannot control the number of the verb.

- When *each, either, every* or *neither* is used as an adjective, the noun it modifies *always* takes a singular verb.

  <u>Every</u> aspect of these charges <u>has been investigated</u>.

- When used as the subject of a sentence, the personal pronoun *it* always takes a singular verb.

  As President Harding reportedly said, <u>it</u> <u>wasn't</u> his enemies who brought him down; <u>it</u> <u>was</u> his friends.

- When the phrase *the number* is the subject of a sentence, it *always* takes a singular verb, no matter the number of the noun in the prepositional phrase.

  <u>The number</u> of unemployment claims <u>is</u> rising.

  Note that *the* is more definite than *a*. *The number* implies an organized unit, which we can take to be singular. *A number* refers to an undefined amount; we don't know how many, but we do know that it is more than one. Therefore, this sentence would be correct:

  <u>A number</u> of masked protestors <u>have arrived</u> at the convention site.

- Definable units of money, measurement, time, organization, food and medical problems *always* take singular verbs.

Twenty thousand dollars is a lot of money.

Four thousand pounds of confiscated marijuana was destroyed in the fire.

(Consider this large amount of marijuana as one giant but singular unit.)

Six hours of waiting has turned anxious parents into angry customers.

The United Auto Workers is poised to strike.

(This is a labor organization, a singular unit.)

Eight ounces of a kale smoothy is her usual breakfast.

Mumps wears down parents as well as children.

- A singular subject followed by such phrases as *together with* and *as well as* always takes a singular verb because those phrases merely modify their subjects.

The tax reduction bill, together with several amendments, has been sent to the president for his signature.

In some cases, *together with* and *as well as* constructions can be awkward. There could be more direct ways to say the same thing.

- When all parts of a compound subject are singular and refer to the *same* person or thing, the verb is *always* singular.

The president and board chair   is Jericho Truett.
     (compound subj.)   (verb)

In this sentence, both of these titles apply to Jericho. A plural verb choice would indicate two people, not one.

The Always Plural Subject

- When a compound subject is joined by the conjunction *and*, it always takes a plural verb if (1) the subjects refer to different persons or things and (2) the subject cannot be considered a unit.

Two partridges and one pear tree were unearthed on the twelfth day of the archeological dig.

Although the part of the compound subject closer to the verb is singular, (tree) the entire subject still takes a plural verb. If it doesn't hurt sentence flow, placing the plural subject closest to the verb may help.

- As the subject of a sentence, indefinite pronouns such as *both, few, many* and *several* always take a plural verb.

Many are cold, but few are frozen.

- Well-recognized foreign plurals require plural verbs if they do not represent a singular unit.

Your criteria for grading my report are unfair.

Criteria, the plural form of *criterion*, means "standards or rules." This word has origins in the Greek language. *Phenomena*, the plural of the Greek *phenomenon*, is another example of plural usage.

Her upper vertebrae were crushed in the accident.

The singular of the Latin-derived *vertebrae* is *vertebra*.

Other so-called foreign plurals include *alumni/alumnae, data, media, memoranda* and *strata*. Not to make you hungry or anything, but *panini* (yum) is an Italian plural.

- The phrase *a number* as the subject takes a plural verb because it does not represent a singular or cohesive unit.

A number of ambitious politicians have arrived at the convention.

Because the actual number of politicians isn't specified, they can't be considered—or treated grammatically—as a singular group. Therefore, it requires a plural verb. Note: this is an example of where a prepositional phrase can influence subject number.

The Singular or Plural Subject

In a few cases, your decision about verb number will be based on the following guidelines, which fortunately have the force of logic behind them. Carefully examine the sentence structure, and you'll do fine.

- When a compound subject contains the conjunction *or* or *but* or contains an *either . . . or* or *neither . . . nor* correlative, the subject *closest* to the verb determines the number of the verb.

Either your nose rings or your eyebrow stud   has to be removed.
         (pl. subj.)   (sing. subj.)   (sing. verb)

The writer might have listed nose rings first to indicate a priority. If no such ranking was intended, then it might have been better to put the singular subject first and the plural one second in order to use a plural verb. It sounds better, too.

Neither <u>he</u> nor the other <u>defendants</u> <u>have entered</u> a plea.
     (sing. subj.)   (pl. subj.)   (pl. verb)

- Depending on their meaning in a sentence, collective nouns and certain words that seem plural in form may take a singular or a plural verb.

Again, the test of a *unit* must be applied. If a word indicates that persons or things are working together as an identifiable unit, the subject must take a singular verb.

Here are some examples of the proper use of the singular verb. We'll follow each example with a plural use when appropriate.

<u>Politics</u> <u>is</u> a topic to avoid at parties.

But note:

The mayor's <u>politics</u> <u>are</u> offensive.

"Practiced political principles" is the meaning here, not the concept of "politics." If you think of this politician as spreading offensive political practices, the meaning becomes clearer.

<u>Acoustics</u> <u>is</u> the scientific study of sound.

But note:

The <u>acoustics</u> in this auditorium <u>are</u> terrible.

Typical collective nouns include *audience, board, crowd, group, herd, public* and *team*. Their intended meanings determine whether such words are intended as singular or plural.

However—and in hopes that it doesn't confuse the issue—the use of a plural verb is correct with what may seem like a collective noun:

The <u>police</u> <u>are</u> on the scene.

It is reasonable to see police here as individuals rather than a collective group, as in the city's **police force <u>is</u>** ...

- Pronouns such as *any, none* and *some* and nouns such as *all* and *most* take singular verbs if they refer to a *unit or a general quantity*. They take plural verbs if they refer to *amount or individuals*.

Not so fast: What about British rules?

If you have traveled in the United Kingdom or enjoyed listening to news from the BBC, no doubt you have seen and heard plural verbs attached to what you consider to be a singular noun. For example, this is common usage in the United Kingdom:

The <u>Parliament</u> are in recess until mid-November.

However, in the U.S. we would write

The <u>Senate</u> <u>is</u> deadlocked over the proposed trade bill.

Simply put, the Brits and their Commonwealth members often "see" individual parts and members in a number of collective nouns, such as team and family. However, you will see singular usage there on occasion when the writer wants to convey a sense of a unified group.

Our view: Let's celebrate differences. We could shift gears now and explain how American spelling "broke away" from British influence, but that's a story for another day.

<u>**All**</u> of the county's <u>farmland</u> <u>is</u> under water.
(unit)

<u>**All**</u> of the <u>crops have been destroyed</u>.
(amount)

<u>**None**</u> of the prosecution <u>witnesses</u> <u>is</u> expected to testify today.
(In this sense, *none* means "not one.")

<u>**None**</u> of the stolen <u>goods were</u> recovered.
(The sentence cannot mean that no one good was recovered; it means that "no goods were recovered.")

None is a particularly maddening pronoun, and its use causes a great deal of debate. However, we believe that the word *none* (meaning "not one") is almost always singular.

- When a subject is a fraction or when it is a word such as *half, part, plenty* and *rest,* its intended number is suggested by the object of the preposition that follows it.

<u>**Three-fourths**</u> of <u>the apartment complex</u> <u>was</u> flooded.
(subj.)   (obj. of prep.)   (verb)

<u>**Three-fourths**</u> of <u>the apartment units</u> <u>were damaged</u>.
(subj.)   (obj. of prep.)   (verb)

Half of the **rent money**   **is** missing.
(subj.)   (obj. of prep.)   (verb)

Half of the **rent receipts**   **are** missing.
(subj.)   (obj. of prep.)   (verb)

Remember, if your sentence seems awkward when you properly employ a rule of agreement, you may want to rewrite it. The use of *none* and of a number of collective nouns may fall into this category. Clarity is your goal.

Identifying subjects by their numbers helps you avoid unnecessary errors. (Quick quiz: Why did we use the singular verb *helps* in the previous sentence? Clue: Remember *gerunds*?)

Pronoun Reference: The Antecedent Search

Pronouns can provide helpful economy to sentences. However, writers should not send readers scrambling to find a pronoun's antecedent because of a confusing reference. So, what *is* an antecedent? It is a noun, either stated or implied, to which that pronoun refers. *Ante* means "before," so the noun precedes (and informs) the pronoun choice.

> **The president has threatened a <u>veto</u>, but the senators don't seem to fear <u>it</u>.**

In the above example, the pronoun *it* obviously refers to *veto*, the antecedent. If the writer had intended to say that the senators feared the president, the appropriate pronoun would have been *him*.

Now, to whom does the pronoun *she* refer in the following sentence?

> **When the officer spotted the robbery suspect in the garage, <u>she</u> quickly ducked behind a pickup truck.**

In this example, you may think it's logical that *she* refers to the officer, who appears to be the main actor in this sentence. Or does *she* mean the robbery suspect? Without a clear connection between pronoun and antecedent, clarity suffers. If your readers search in vain for a clear reference for the pronoun, you have engaged in a false economy. It's time to for more detail:

> **Officer Bill Morehouse entered the garage and spotted the robbery suspect, who quickly ducked behind a pickup truck.**

A more difficult problem with pronouns is number and person agreement with antecedents. Consider these sentences:

Zanne is the <u>only one</u> of our doctoral students <u>who has</u> received a fellowship in her third year of study.

In this sentence, the proximity of the noun *students* to the relative pronoun *who* might suggest that *who* refers to the plural *students*. In fact, only one student—Zanne—has "received a fellowship." Plus, the possessive pronoun *her* provides another clue. Hence, we use the singular verb *has received*.

Now consider this sentence:

He is one of the funniest comedians who have appeared in Las Vegas.

Now—"He" is not *the* funniest; he is among a group (small, large?) of very funny comics. Hence, a plural verb is needed. And, yes, in this case the object of a preposition (*comedians*) suggests the number of the relative pronoun *that*, which is the subject of its clause.

The <u>logic</u> of his arguments cannot support <u>itself</u>.

Support of the arguments' logic, not the arguments themselves, is the topic of this sentence. Hence, the singular *logic* is followed by the singular pronoun *itself*, rather than *themselves*.

The sales manager's <u>presentation</u> was flashy, but not many buyers
(antecedent)

were swayed by <u>it</u>.
(pronoun)

Don't be fooled by the possessive *manager's*. Obviously, it modifies *presentation*.

<u>Neither</u> of the men has admitted <u>his</u> involvement in the burglary.
(subj.)   (pron.)

As you recall, *neither* takes a singular verb. It follows that the possessive pronoun *his*, referring to *neither*, would have to be singular as well.

Remember, a pronoun must agree with its antecedent in both number and person.

Case: It's All About Relationships

Decisions, decisions: Is it *he, him* or *his*? Is it *who, whom* or *whose*?

These questions deal with *case*, the forms that *pronouns* take depending on *their* role in a sentence. (Did you note the proper antecedent agreement in the previous sentence?) Case contributes to sentence harmony by maintaining proper grammatical relationships. These relationships require a change in form for pronouns in three instances and for nouns in only one.

We'll focus primarily on pronouns in this section, with a brief mention of the one area of case that affects the noun. Chapter 7 (on punctuation) will discuss how nouns change in the possessive case.

Pronouns have three forms: *nominative* (also known as *subjective*), *objective* and *possessive*. The relative pronoun *who* and the personal pronoun *she* illustrate these forms.

- Nominative, as the subject of the sentence:

  <u>Who</u> left this apartment in such a mess?

  Tom and <u>she</u> agreed to sign the apartment lease.

- Objective, as the object or receiver of action:

  <u>Whom</u> did the committee select as its spokesperson?

  Remember, subjects aren't always at the beginning of a sentence. Here, the subject is *committee*, which makes *whom* the direct object of the verb *select*.

  This should be an easy assignment for <u>her</u>.

  In this sentence, *her* is the object of the preposition *for*.

- Possessive, to modify a noun:

  It's uncertain <u>whose</u> essay will win the competition.

  Whose (not *who's*), the possessive form of *who*, modifies the noun *essay*.

  The chancellor said the decision to proceed was <u>hers</u>.

  Hers (not *her's*) modifies the noun *decision*.

All this may seem straightforward, but unfortunately, errors in case usage are distressingly common. For example:

Between you and <u>I</u>, this will be a close game.

Here the writer fails to use objective case *me* as object of preposition *between*.

<u>Her</u> and I are going to the mall today.

Her is in the objective case in this erroneous sentence, yet it is acting as a subject—and so, of course, it must be in the nominative case, *she*. This not-uncommon error reflects a lack of understanding of subject and object in a sentence.

Nominative Case

Think "subject" when you consider the nominative case. Nominative relates directly to the subject of a sentence and to any pronoun that refers to that subject. So, a subject, the predicate nominative of a linking verb (p. 41), and a subject's *appositive* (a word, phrase or clause related to the subject) *all* are in the nominative case.

The nominative case of the personal pronoun includes *I, you, he/she/ it, we, you* and *they*. The relative pronoun *who* is also in the nominative case.

Some examples:

<u>She</u> refuses to testify for the prosecution.

It was <u>he</u> who turned in the alarm.

The pronoun *he* is in the nominative case as the predicate nominative of the linking verb *was*. This sounds pretty formal, we know, but you can understand the meaning that *he* called the police. In truth, such constructions are rarely used in everyday writing.

<u>We</u> dreamers still have to work.

The pronoun *we* is supplemented, or "complemented," by *dreamers*, which makes that noun an appositive. So, both *we* and *dreamers* serve as subject of the sentence. Therefore, *we* is in the nominative case.

Remember that each clause requires a subject. In complex and compound-complex sentences (see p. 27), each pronoun that serves as a clause's subject must be in the nominative case.

Use of nominative with linking verbs

It's me.

That's him.

These sentences have been acceptable in colloquial speech for years and so you may be unhappily surprised to learn that they are ungrammatical.

It is I is the correct construction. Don't worry: We are not suggesting that you start talking this way. We are suggesting, however, that writing demands an adherence to grammatical rules that casual speech does not.

The following sentence is precise—and correct:

It was <u>she</u> who refused to testify.

Because the pronoun *she* follows a linking verb, you might be tempted to think it belongs in the objective case. It doesn't. *She* is renaming or further defining the subject, *it*. Keep in mind that such a construction is not a paragon of clear, concise writing; it is more direct to say:

<u>She</u> refused to testify.

or, for more precision and detail:

Helen Thompson, who is facing prosecution in a separate trial, refused to testify yesterday in the racketeering trial of Vic Hugo.

Selecting *who* in complex constructions

Most of us have little difficulty recognizing the correct use of *who* when it is the simple subject of a simple clause. *Whom* (in the objective case), however, is another matter—and an example of how usage and rules may change over time.

First, a look at who:

Presidential adviser Frank Henson, <u>who</u> reportedly leaked the confidential report on health care costs, has resigned.

But when the true subject *who* is separated from its verb, the possibility of case error increases. Note this *incorrect* example:

The adviser <u>whom</u> the president said had leaked the confidential report has resigned.

Whom is not the object of *the president said*. The sentence can be analyzed this way to show why the correct choice is *who:*

The adviser ... has resigned
(independent clause)

who ... had leaked
(dependent clause)

the president said
(parenthetical information to provide a source)

As you recall from our earlier discussion, you must match the number of the subject to the proper verb. You must also select the right case if the subject is a pronoun:

<u>Who</u> did he say won the race?
(*Who won* the race, he did say.)

Who/Whom in prepositional phrases

A pronoun in a prepositional phrase is always in the objective case because it is generally the object of a preposition, as in "To whom did you wish to speak?" But there are exceptions when a preposition controls an entire clause.

Sometimes a preposition will be a linking device, much like a conjunction or a relative pronoun. Look to the clause that follows to determine whether the pronoun is acting as subject or object:

The radio station will award $5,000 in cash <u>to whoever</u> submits
(independent clause)   (pronoun in nom. case)

the first correct answer to its "mystery question."

Although the object of a preposition takes the objective case in a simple phrase, the presence of an entire clause connected to the preposition changes the rules. All clauses need a subject, either stated or implied. Hence, we use *whoever* in the preceding sentence as the subject of the clause (using the preposition *to* as a linking device).

You can be more direct, however, by starting the sentence with *whoever:*

<u>Whoever</u> answers the radio station's "mystery question" first will win $5,000. (Note that we trimmed eight words from the original!)

Here's another example:

He discussed the end of the world <u>with whoever</u> would listen.

Note the two clauses:

<u>He</u> discussed/<u>whoever</u> would listen.

Case in *than* clauses

Remember our discussion of comparatives in Chapter 5? Case is an important component in certain clauses when these comparisons are being made, as in this sentence:

She is stronger <u>than I</u>.

Than is frequently a conjunction. As you'll recall, conjunctions connect whole clauses and phrases. Because the second clause in a comparison is often implied, you must mentally complete the thought to determine proper case:

She is stronger than I (am strong).

In this sentence, the nominative case *I* is required because that pronoun is the subject of the implied clause.

Than can also be a preposition, however, as in this example:

There is no better snowboarder than <u>her</u>.

You can see that *than* is not a conjunction here because in this sentence the comparison ends with *her*. Remember that you can give comparative and superlative degrees to adjectives and adverbs, but not to nouns. So, it doesn't make sense to complete the thought:

There is no better snowboarder <u>than she is a snowboarder</u>.

Objective Case

Personal pronouns (*I, you, he, she, it, we, you, they*) and the relative and in-terrogative pronoun *who* also change form when used in the objective case.

	Personal Pronouns	**Relative or Interrogative Pronoun**
Singular:	me, you, him/her/it	whom
Plural:	us, you, them	whom

Personal pronouns in the objective case have the following uses:

- As the direct or indirect object of a verb or verbal:

  Oprah accompanied <u>him</u> to the premiere.
            (dir. obj.)

  County commissioners gave <u>her</u> a <u>10 percent raise</u>.
            (indir. obj.)   (dir. obj.)

  Giving <u>them</u> a raise at this time sends the wrong message.
         (object of verbal)

  (Note from our discussion on p. 46 that this verbal phrase is the subject of the sentence.)

- As the object of a preposition:

  <u>Between you and me</u>, he won't be around here for long.
  (prep.)   (obj. of prep.)

  Harold says there is no better lacrosse player than <u>her</u>.
  (preposition and object)

  Remember that while adjectives and adverbs can be compared, nouns can't.

- With an appositive that is in the objective case:

  Guards dragged <u>us reporters</u> out of the convention hall.

  The pronoun *us* and its appositive *reporters* function as one unit—the direct object.

  She gave the cleaning job <u>to us students</u>.

  The pronoun *us* and appositive *students* are part of the object of the preposition *to*.

Horton rarely hears a WHOM (apologies to Dr. Seuss)

One of the social and cultural debates going on in grammar and writing today deals with the *who/whom* choice, in which tradition battles contemporary usage. Some talking points, gathered from our observation of usage from many quarters:

1. *Who* is easier to use than whom.

2. *Whom* is seen by some (many) as formal and stuffy.

3. The "*whom*" choice is really hard!

As you will see in the following section, the proper use of *whom* simply requires an understanding of sentence structure, which is thoroughly discussed in Chapter 3. That said, we do recognize that *whom* is rapidly disappearing in everyday speech, and we even see some abandonment of it in some news and public relations writing. It has virtually disappeared from advertising (you figure out why).

However, it still exists in most professional writing, as it should. So, let's examine how to properly employ *whom*. And for starters, don't ever start a letter with "To WHO it may concern."

Channeling the spirit of Horton, that determined elephant, "we meant what we said, and we said what we meant."

The proper use of *whom*

The relative and interrogative pronoun *who* changes to *whom* in the objective case. The *who/whom* choice becomes easier if you carefully analyze the sentence. Let's look at a few examples.

<u>Whom</u> do <u>you</u> wish to see?
(dir. obj.)   (subj.)

Remember that a direct object doesn't always follow the subject and verb. It can appear before the subject.

Now consider this sentence with two clauses:

She is the only candidate <u>whom</u> the union supports.

First, identify the two subjects, two verbs, one predicate nominative and one direct object in this sentence:

<u>She</u>	<u>is</u> the only <u>candidate</u>	the <u>union</u> <u>supports</u> whom
(subj.)	(verb) (pred. nom.)	(subj.) (verb) (dir. object)

So, we have two clauses—one independent, one dependent. The second clause as rewritten clearly shows *whom* (objective case) as a direct object.

However, here's an issue of conciseness to consider: It would be even smoother (and equally correct) to write:

> **She is the only candidate the union supports.**

So—do you know *whom* to contact in the event of a grammatical crisis?

Possessive Case

Personal pronouns have these possessive forms:

my	mine	our	ours	your	yours
his	her	hers	its	their	theirs

As you can see, an apostrophe is not used with personal pronouns. However, some indefinite pronouns, such as *another, anyone, everyone, everybody, one* and *someone* do require an apostrophe in their possessive forms.

Here are two examples, all connected with the noun *book*:

> **Is it <u>your</u> book?**

> **Yes, it is <u>mine</u>.**

And note the punctuation, however, with the indefinite pronoun *someone:*

> **This must be <u>someone's</u> book!**

Nouns change only in the possessive case

Case is less complicated for nouns because they change only in their possessive form. When a noun changes to a possessive, it requires an apostrophe; that is not true for most pronouns. Here is an example of the correct use of both a noun possessive and the possessive of the pronoun *it:*

> **The <u>president's</u> speech was notable for <u>its</u> warning to tax dodgers.**
> (noun—poss.)   (pronoun—poss.)

"Possessing" a gerund

When a personal pronoun modifies a gerund in a sentence, the possessive case is used to show possession or ownership by the gerund, which is **always** a noun.

> **I will not tolerate <u>his</u> <u>reacting</u> that way during our meetings.**
> (pron.) (gerund phrase as direct object)

In this sentence, *his* modifies the gerund *reacting,* which is the direct object of the verb tolerate. Because a gerund is a noun, it is necessary to use its pronoun in the possessive case.

The *who/whose* relationship

The *relative* pronoun *who* also has a possessive form: *whose.* It does not take an apostrophe even though it modifies a noun:

Yes, she's the filmmaker <u>whose</u> documentary took top honors at Sundance.

The *interrogative* pronoun *who* also uses *whose* as its possessive form:

<u>Whose</u> film will win the Oscar?

Some writers struggle with the *who's/whose* distinction. Like *it's, who's* is a *contraction*—a compression of two words (in this case, *who is*). It is a subject and a verb, not a possessive. If you can read *to whom* into a sentence with your *whose* selection, you're on the right track:

<u>Whose</u> pastrami <u>sandwich</u> is this? (<u>To whom</u> does this sandwich
(possessive)   (subject)
belong?)

<u>Who's</u> responsible for this mess? (<u>Who is</u> responsible. . . .)
(subj.–verb)

More about contractions

Contractions can be troublesome with personal pronouns as well. The most common errors involve misuse of *its/it's, your/you're* and *their/they're.* Note these correct usages for this trio:

The unemployment rate has fallen to <u>its</u> lowest level in three years.
(possessive)

"<u>It's</u> about time," he muttered.
(contraction of *it* and *is*)

<u>Your</u> report was eaten by my dog.
(possessive)

<u>You're</u> up next!
(contraction of *you* and *are*)

<u>Their</u> decision will be announced on Monday.
(possessive)

Paul and Paula say <u>they're</u> ready to take the plunge.
(contraction of *they* and *are*)

Be sure to keep this sentence in mind as you consider *they're/there/their* choices:

<u>They're</u> convinced <u>there</u> are no obstacles to <u>their</u> success.

We hope you can see how case is connected to agreement—and to harmony. Proper use of case adds clarity to your writing. It reflects an attention to detail.

Parallel Structure

The final part of our discussion of agreement focuses on balance and order. A sentence is considered *parallel* when its various units are in proper rhythm. When a sentence lacks parallelism, its focus softens and its rhythm falters.

Parallelism is both a grammatical concern and a stylistic issue. (You'll read more about parallelism and style in Chapter 9.) However, parallelism does not imply *rigidity*—it simply means that there is coherence in both structure and meaning. Let's examine the most typical problems in parallelism.

Common errors in parallelism

1. Creating a series that is unbalanced and awkward:

He enjoys <u>football,</u> <u>movies</u> and <u>riding around in his dune buggy</u>.

Why is this sentence unbalanced? It contains three nouns in a series, but the third noun is a verbal (gerund). It throws off the meter; it lacks parallel structure. You can regain rhythm by using three gerund phrases:

He enjoys <u>playing football,</u> <u>watching movies</u> and <u>riding his dune buggy</u>.

In the next example, an adjective clashes with a prepositional phrase in a brief series:

Your report is comprehensive and of an <u>innovative nature</u>.
(adjective)   (prepositional phrase)

Fix this easily with two simple adjectives, which also creates a more concise thought:

Your report is <u>comprehensive</u> and <u>innovative</u>.
(adj.)   (adj.)

2. Mixing verbals

This is another example of selectively <u>using favorable statistics</u>
(gerund phrase)

and then <u>to write a report</u> around that biased selection.
(infinitive phrase)

Here, the gerund and infinitive phrases conflict. The sentence would be parallel if the writer stuck with gerunds. Note how the rhythm seems more natural in this version:

This is another example of selectively <u>using favorable statistics</u> and <u>writing a report</u> around that biased selection.

3. Unnecessarily changing voice

Verbs can have active or passive voices (see p. 33). Writers choose a voice according to the need to have the subject perform the action or to have it acted upon. Shifting voice can disrupt the flow of a construction, as in this example:

<u>The City Council easily approved</u> the rezoning ordinance, but <u>a</u>
(active voice)
<u>property tax amnesty proposal was rejected</u> by the council with a
(passive voice)
resounding "no" vote.

This awkward, unnecessarily wordy sentence uses two subjects and switches from active to passive voice. Be direct and concise: stick with the same subject and voice:

The City Council <u>easily approved</u> the rezoning ordinance but <u>resoundingly rejected</u> a property tax amnesty proposal.

Both verbs are in the active voice now. Note, too, the improvement in rhythm. The edited version is smooth and coherent.

4. Unnecessarily changing subjects

<u>One</u> never should argue with an umpire; <u>players</u> should know that by now.

Besides creating a stilted construction with both singular and plural subjects, the writer is also wasting words. The sentence would read better with just one focused subject:

<u>Players</u> should know by now never to argue with an umpire.

A Final Note

We hope that we have "made the case for agreement" because we believe your writing is more effective when it is free of elements that interrupt harmony and balance. Your readers should not struggle to understand your meaning—so provide them with a smooth journey as they enjoy your work.

For additional resources go to **www.cengagebrain.com**

Punctuation: Your Symphony of Signals and Stops

7

We salute the punctuation mark—a symbol of authority and civility. With underappreciated grace, it helps us to stop, pause, link ideas, create an aside or prepare for a question or an emphatic retort. It does this with the most diminutive of devices—among them, the period and the comma—to help readers see and feel a writer's pace. They are, indeed, wondrous dots and dashes and typographical curlicues.

To some folks, the misuse of a punctuation mark is tantamount to abuse. For example, The Apostrophe Protection Society was founded in England more than a decade ago to politely point out to offenders that a store sign such as "The Elephants Trunk" was in desperate need of an apostrophe to show true possession. Similar groups also exist in the United States, some more guerilla-like than others.

Our view is that proper punctuation brings order and coherence to writing. Just as composers use a system of marks to note the speed and rhythm of music, writers use punctuation to provide a system of stops and starts, of controlled pauses and of forward motion. The right amount of punctuation works quietly in the background, with grace and elegance, to clarify ideas and determine content exactly as the writer intends.

Some Basic Guidelines

Let's begin with a quick overview of our punctuation system.

- A *period* ends a sentence.

- A *comma*, however, creates a short pause within a sentence.

- A *semicolon* slows the reader within the sentence; it isn't powerful enough to signal a complete stop.

- A *colon* announces the following: a list, a fragment, a sentence or a quotation.

- A *dash*—maligned by purists but used frequently in journalism—creates a more abrupt break than a comma.

- *Quotation marks* are dedicated "record keepers." They announce somebody's exact words, signify titles of short works and indicate nicknames, among other things.

- A *hyphen* is well-used in our language. It joins modifiers that belong together.

- An *apostrophe* is grammar's helper with subject–verb contractions and with proper indication of the possessive case.

- An *ellipsis* warns us ... something is missing.

- *Parentheses*, they look like this, ( ), are used to clarify a point or add an aside without (we hope) hampering sentence rhythm. We'll also include a discusion [sic] of brackets in that section.

- Do you really need an explanation of the *question mark*?

- If you do, we shall indicate our astonishment with another way to end a sentence—the *exclamation point*!

Period

The period is the "closer." It signals that the action of one sentence has stopped before the next begins. Imagine how confusing sentences would be without periods:

> **Snow and gale-force winds cut a deadly swath across two states yesterday police reported today that more than 2,000 vehicles were stranded overnight freezing temperatures tonight are expected to create even dire conditions, according to emergency officials**

Proper periods would have created three concise sentences here. Without them, we have trouble sorting out concepts as well as complete thoughts.

The period has two main uses in writing.

1. Use a period to end a sentence that is neither interrogative (?) nor exclamatory (!).

   His boss persuaded Nathan to take a vacation.

2. Use a period to create certain abbreviations and to indicate decimals.

The $2.5-million package arrived C.O.D. at the home office.

Abbreviations are space savers, and periods help signal these shortcuts. Not all abbreviations, however, require periods. Acronyms (abbreviations without punctuation, which are pronounceable words—for example, *UNESCO* and *AIDS*), names of certain organizations and government agencies (*NBC, UAW, FBI* and *CIA*) and abbreviations of technical words (*mph* and *rpm*)— do not require periods. To learn which abbreviations use periods and which ones don't, consult a dictionary or your publication's stylebook.

Comma

The comma is vital to a sentence's circulation of ideas. That sentence stumbles with too many commas; with too few, those ideas may suffer a confusing collision. Let's examine proper use of the comma and then look at some of its inappropriate uses. Note: The comma is notorious for its misuse, so please examine this section carefully.

- Use a comma to separate two independent clauses connected by a coordinating conjunction.

  I like my army of punctuation marks, <u>and</u> I'm sure they really like me.

  Coordinating conjunctions include *or, and, nor, but, yet* and *so*. A comma is placed before the coordinating conjunction to link two independent clauses that can stand alone as complete sentences. Journalistic style favors dropping the comma if both independent clauses of the sentence are short and uncomplicated (with no long prepositional or dependent clauses, for instance), and meaning is unambiguous:

  Prefontaine lost a shoe but he kept running.

- Use a comma to set off long introductory clauses and phrases and some *shorter* clauses and phrases that would be confusing without it.

  After the smoke alarm went off for the third time in two hours, the hotel clerk finally called the fire department.

  To Meryl Streep, Oscar is a familiar name.

  You can omit the comma for some short clauses and phrases if no run-on occurs in the sentence—that is, if the meaning of the introductory segment remains distinct from the rest of the sentence. For example, a comma would be unnecessary here:

In winter we often dream of scorching sun and coconut oil.

- Use commas to set off nonrestrictive (nonessential) clauses, phrases and modifiers from the rest of the sentence.

This is an appropriate place to explain the distinctions between nonrestrictive and restrictive clauses and how the comma signals these differences.

Nonrestrictive (Nonessential)

Nonrestrictive clauses, phrases and words require commas because they are *incidental* to the sentence. That is, those elements could be removed from the sentence with little if any loss to meaning or context.

The senator, <u>who travels on her own plane</u>, will visit nine senior centers in three states this weekend to talk about the Affordable Care Act.

Sentence meaning remains the same when the underlined subordinate clause is removed. (The senator's transportation choice is not key to the meaning of the sentence.)

Restrictive (Essential)

Clauses, phrases or words that are essential to the meaning of the sentence are called *restrictive*. They need not be set off with commas from the rest of the sentence. Notice how this example differs from the nonrestrictive constructions:

The three men <u>who hijacked a city bus</u> died when they crashed it into a police blockade.

The subordinate clause *who hijacked a city bus* limits the meaning of the sentence. One test to determine restrictive meaning is to read the sentence without the clause in question. If you find yourself trying to fill in the meaning of the sentence, that clause is essential. Consider this sentence, a compressed version of the previous example:

The three men died when they crashed into a police blockade.

This clearly requires its accompanying clause to make the sentence more complete, more understandable. (What men? What did they do?) For this reason the clause *who hijacked a city bus* should not be set off by commas.
Here's another example:

The water main <u>that broke last night</u> flooded the entire southeast side of the city.

Not all water mains broke last night. Because the subordinate clause *that broke last night* is essential to the meaning of the sentence, no commas should be used.

Note that in a restrictive clause the pronoun *that* is used instead of *which*. If the clause is not essential to the meaning of the sentence but simply provides added detail, use *which* and set off the clause with commas. (See the entry in Part 2 for *that/which/who.*)

- Use commas to separate items in a series.

Samantha stuffed seven pebbles, three cookies and two frogs in her pocket.

Journalistic writing favors this rule for use of the *serial comma*: When the last item in a series is connected by a coordinating conjunction, the comma should be omitted before that conjunction. This is especially true when the series is short or uncomplicated. If the series is made up of more than simple adjective–noun combinations, however, the comma can be inserted before the conjunction to eliminate confusion:

Union officials this morning said they would bargain vigorously for the right to negotiate pension fund investments, an expanded process of grievance procedures, and binding arbitration for all contract matters not settled within 90 days of the start of negotiations.

Although rare in journalistic writing, the serial comma appears more frequently in formal composition, novels and academic texts.

- Use commas to separate descriptive modifiers of equal rank.

When a noun is preceded by a string of adjectives, apply this two-part test to determine whether those modifiers are equal: Can you use these adjectives interchangeably? Can you successfully insert the conjunction *and* between them and have the sentence make sense? If so, these adjectives are coordinate and require a comma.

Given this test, the modifiers in the following sentence need a comma:

Her talk show turned into a frantic, irrational gabfest.

You can read "frantic *and* irrational" into this sentence, so the comma is necessary.

Meteorologists forecast another cold, dreary Midwestern night.

You can read "cold *and* dreary" into this sentence. They modify *Midwestern night* equally, so they are considered coordinate. The comma is necessary.

But what about this sentence?

Meteorologists forecast another <u>frosty Midwestern</u> night.

You can't read "frosty *and* Midwestern night" into this construction, so the adjectives need not be separated by a comma. In fact, *frosty* actually modifies *Midwestern night.*

- Use commas to set off parenthetical expressions.

A *parenthetical expression* is an addition or "aside" to the main thought. It gives extra information without disrupting the flow of the sentence:

The first day of the bird-watching season, <u>often a flurry of activity</u>, was unusually quiet this year.

The snow, <u>encrusted with a thin skin of ice</u>, crunched lightly under her boots.

The underlined phrase could be put in parentheses, but that might be too formal and stilted. Commas create shorter pauses while maintaining the flow.

- Use commas when the absence of a pause can cause confusion.

<u>For the senator,</u> <u>going fishing</u> for three hours is vacation enough.

<u>Circling the brewery, workers</u> silently protested their working conditions.

In the preceding examples, it would be a false economy to waive comma use. The pause is necessary for clarity.

- Use commas to set off participial phrases that modify some part of the independent clause.

The Senate adjourned today, <u>having defeated an attempt to</u>
(participial phrase modifies *Senate*)
<u>extend the session.</u>

Various stylebooks list many other examples of comma use (and nonuse). Some may be obvious to you:

- To separate numbers in the thousands and above: 7,240 entries.

- To distinguish a city from its state: He lives in Cleveland, Ohio.

- To separate direct address from a sentence: Ozzie, will you answer the door?

Comma Misuse

The comma is designed to improve the flow of prose, but errant commas impede it. Here are some helpful points to prevent comma misuse.

- *Do not use a comma* to separate two independent clauses that are *not* joined by a coordinating conjunction.

  Violating this rule produces the *comma* splice and creates a *run-on sentence*. It looks like this:

  The unemployment rate continues to fall, the rate of inflation is increasing.

Using a comma to link two independent clauses (which could stand alone as separate sentences) offers an inadequate pause in thought and causes a *run-on sentence*. We recommend that you either break the sentence in two or do one of the following:

1. Use a semicolon instead of a comma to link the clauses.

2. Better suggestion: Add a coordinating conjunction with a comma.

   The unemployment rate continues to fall, <u>but</u> the rate of inflation is increasing.

- Do not use a comma to separate a compound predicate.

  A compound predicate (two or more verbs that serve the same subject) does not need a comma because it is part of the same clause:

  The <u>judge</u>   <u>fined</u> the men $500 and   <u>ordered</u> them to perform
  (subj.)   (verb #1)   (verb #2)

  40 hours of community service.

  As you can see, "The judge" has performed two actions within the same clause, making this construction a simple sentence.

- Do not use a comma to introduce a dependent clause.

  The use of a comma before *because* is one of the biggest offenders. *Because* is a *subordinating conjunction*—it introduces a dependent clause that cannot stand alone:

  The studio executive rejected the movie idea because she wanted a guaranteed blockbuster.

  No comma is needed here because the conjunction does not coordinate equal clauses. (Did you notice the lack of a comma in the previous sentence as well?) That is why *and*, *but* and *or* often require commas; they are called *coordinating conjunctions* because they link clauses of equal weight.

Note that if the subordinate clause is used at the beginning of the sentence, a comma is required:

Because he wanted a guaranteed blockbuster, the studio executive rejected the movie idea.

Can you detect a difference in rhythm between *because* at the beginning of a sentence and *because* in the middle of it?

- Do not use a comma to separate a subject from its predicate or object.

This is one of the most common errors made by inexperienced writers. Sentences with restrictive clauses, phrases or words between the subject and the predicate sometimes confuse writers into putting a comma before the predicate. Even relatively simple subjects fall prey to this error.

The dangerous inmate, escaped today in a delivery truck.

Knowing rules of grammar, will ensure your credibility as a writer.

In the preceding examples, the comma is unnecessary. Always be sure the subject of the sentence has a clear, unobstructed route to its predicate when restrictive (essential) elements mark the pathway.

- Do not use a comma between a word and a phrase that amplifies it if it will create a "false series."

This sentence, as punctuated, is bound to cause confusion:

Rescuers discovered seven bodies, four office workers, two firefighters and one police officer.

Unless the writer meant to say that 14 people were discovered and that seven of them were dead, the comma use after *bodies* is wrong. A colon or dash would be more effective in separating the two ideas:

Rescuers discovered seven bodies—those of four office workers, two firefighters and one police officer.

- Do not use a comma to precede a partial quotation.

The mayor says his opponent is "a rat dressed in weasel's clothing."

No comma is needed after *is* because the quoted material is the predicate nominative of the verb *is*. Because the quoted material depends on the rest of the sentence for its context, that material should not be set off by a comma.

If the quotation is a full sentence, however, it should be preceded by a comma:

The defense attorney asked, "How would you like to go to prison for a crime you didn't commit?"

Remember: Good writers use commas for clarity and meter. If your sentences contain a clutter of commas, take heed. Perhaps the sentences are too long and too busy. There is grace and order in simplicity and conciseness.

Semicolon

The *semicolon* indicates a longer pause than a comma, but not the full stop of a period. Because it carries a grammatical formality that some writers like to avoid, the semicolon is used infrequently in media writing.

Writers sometimes opt for two separate and shorter sentences rather than joining two independent clauses with a semicolon. They may choose to break up a series of thoughts normally punctuated by semicolons to avoid long clauses and phrases. But the semicolon is effective when the writer wants the chime of one idea to fall away for a beat before the next rings out—a lingering that is absent with a period.

Here are four guidelines to help you properly employ the semicolon.

- Use a semicolon to join independent clauses *not connected* by a coordinating conjunction.

  Sarah will contest the election <u>results</u>; <u>she</u> says she will accept the outcome of a "properly supervised" recount.

  If those two clauses had been connected with the coordinating conjunction *but*, a comma would have sufficed:

  ... election results, but she says she ...

Some writers prefer the use of the coordinating conjunction because it gives more specific direction to the reader. Others would look at these two long clauses and break them into two sentences.

Words like *however, moreover, nevertheless* and *therefore* are not coordinating conjunctions. They are *conjunctive adverbs*. They do not perform the linking function of a conjunction and cannot coordinate clauses of equal rank. When a conjunctive adverb separates two independent clauses, a semicolon is required.

  I understand the main points of your argument; however, I don't agree with your conclusion.

- Use a semicolon to link more than two independent clauses in a series.

Semicolons are used in compound sentences when more than two independent clauses are linked in a series—even when the last part of the series is connected by a coordinating conjunction. However, this use is rare in media writing; we show you the example below just to indicate its proper punctuation.

> **We will find proper funding for our <u>schools</u>; <u>we</u> will not abandon our commitment to greater access to higher <u>education</u>; <u>and</u> we will press for a new income tax measure to fully fund our programs.**

- Use a semicolon to separate internally punctuated independent clauses joined by a coordinating conjunction.

When you punctuate a clause internally with commas, you can't use a comma to separate that clause from another. A semicolon is needed to create a more abrupt stop:

> **The city council has approved the proposed levy, which will go to voters in May; but the mayor has indicated that she will campaign against it.**

- Use a semicolon to set off parts of a series that also contain commas.

> **Survivors of the early-morning crash are Stan Sarsgaard, 42, of San Francisco; his brother-in-law, Martin Fedler, 40, of Boise, Idaho; and their guide, Deb Walters, 30, of Fairbanks, Alaska.**

The main function of the semicolon in this example is effective organization. It is helpful because it clarifies boundaries in a series better than a comma so that the parts remain distinct.

To recap: The semicolon is generally used in more formal writing. However, in all forms, the semicolon creates a more distinct break in thought without bringing the sentence to a complete stop. It is essential in joining independent clauses that are not connected with a coordinating conjunction.

Colon

The *colon* is an elegant announcer: It ushers in complete sentences, lists, quotations and dialogue.

Proper Use of the Colon

When the colon is used to introduce a lengthy sentence, the first word of that sentence should be capitalized:

> **Here's a novel idea: Proofread your work if you expect to have it (and you) taken seriously.**

When a colon is used to introduce a word, phrase or a clause that is not part of a complete sentence, the first word following the colon *should not* be capitalized:

In the movie classic "The Graduate," Dustin Hoffman learned the one word that would guarantee a successful future: *plastics*.

Note these other functions of the colon:

- Use a colon to introduce a quotation that is longer than one sentence.

  The judge eyed the defendant and told him in words dripping with disdain: "Your disgusting conduct in my courtroom has mocked everything that is justice. I now invite you to accept our jail hospitality for the next 90 days."

- Use a colon to end a sentence that introduces a quotation in the next paragraph.

  Here is the text of the president's speech:

  "Good evening, my fellow Americans. I appear before you tonight to report on the state of our nation."

- Use colons to show the text of questions and answers.

  This can take two forms:

  Q: And then what happened?

  A: She put the meat cleaver down and called the cops.

  As you can see, the colon eliminates the need for quotation marks unless the dialogue itself quotes other material.

- Use colons to show times and citations.

  Lauren ran the mile in 3:49:42.

  Psalm 101:5 warns of the danger of slander.

When Not to Use the Colon

- Do not use a colon when introducing a short list without the words *the following*.

  The voters have elected Larry, Curly and Moe.

- Do not use a colon when introducing a direct quotation of one sentence or less. A comma is sufficient.

  Bogie told her, "I'll see you when I see you."

- Do not use a colon to separate an independent clause from a prepositional phrase that begins with *including*.

Please have all of the assistant professors report to me, including that no-good Billy Smithers.

The proper punctuation mark to use before *including* is a comma.

Dash

Some cynics contend that journalists invented the dash—that wisp of punctuation longer than a hyphen, more direct than parentheses and far more casual than a colon—to intrude with an abrupt but important thought. In truth, the primary uses of a *dash* are to signal a change of direction and to create emphasis. Journalists, however, can be rightfully accused of using the dash to excess or of using it when a comma, a colon or parentheses might be more skillfully employed. The dash should be used sparingly; it loses its impact with too frequent use. Let's look at the two main uses of the dash in all writing.

- Use a dash to end a sentence with a surprising or ironic element.

The tall, distinguished-looking man entered the country with a valid passport, two pieces of leather luggage, an antique Leica camera around his neck—and 16 ounces of uncut heroin in the heels of his alligator boots.

A comma here would not be as effective in changing meter and warning the reader of a break in thought.

A simple comma suffices when an abrupt or surprising break is not needed:

Baker, the Giant's defensive genius, hurled a rifle shot from right field to cut down a speeding Thomas at home plate.

- Use dashes to set off a long clause or a phrase that is in apposition to the main clause, when it makes the information clearer and more distinctive.

The closing ceremonies of the Olympics—a dazzling spectacle of unabashed self-promotion—set off an explosion of self-congratulations at the network.

A comma usually suffices with a shorter appositive:

Barry Nelson, heir to the Smoothware fortune, is not noted for his philanthropy.

Dashes could also be used to set off both parenthetical expressions and a series of items in the middle of a sentence. We recommend restraint with these uses, however, and that you concentrate on the two main uses of the dash.

Quotation Marks

Quotation marks have several identities. They speak truth when they give a faithful reproduction of what was said. They can also attack and belittle. For example, what impressions do quotation marks create in these sentences?

"I believe we can correct this situation," the accountant said.

This seems to be a straightforward recounting of what was said.

The company spokesperson said her firm could correct the "situation."

Placement of quotation marks around *situation* makes us suspicious. What is so strange about this so-called situation? The quotation marks alert us to the possibility of another meaning.

Let's look at the appropriate use of quotation marks in writing and then see how other marks of punctuation are used with quotations.

Proper Use of Quotation Marks

- Use quotation marks to enclose direct quotations and to capture dialog.

  "We have three months to complete construction of our new plant, or our bond rate will be in jeopardy," Board President Sandy Jay said.

  "So, did you actually see a weapon?" the defense attorney asked.

  "No. Well, I thought I did," the defendant replied.

  "I'll take that as a no."

  Avoid the unnecessary use of partial quotations. Sometimes a paraphrase will do. So, instead of:

  Clarkson CEO Andrew Bentley said this morning that "profits will increase" in the third quarter thanks to "better control of expenditures."

you might write:

Clarkson's third-quarter profits will increase because of better expenditure control, CEO Andrew Bentley said this morning.

The partial quotation works best if the language or style of what is quoted is distinctive or colorful. For example, it would be difficult to paraphrase this effectively:

Sen. Paul Nelson, D-Hood River, compared the higher-education system to a dinosaur that's "going to fall in the tar pits and become a fossil."

Avoid putting quotation marks around single words if their use results in an inaccurate representation. We generally put these marks around unfamiliar terms on first reference, around slang words and around words used sarcastically or ironically. But don't overdo it!

A wage freeze is in effect.

but

His luck ran into a "freeze" at the track.

Vanessa Truett's dreams are a $20-million business.

but

Tom Anderson's "dreams" have ruined those of elderly investors who spent their life savings on his worthless pyramid scheme.

- Use quotation marks for titles of books, lectures, movies, operas, plays, poems, songs, speeches, television shows and works of art. This follows AP style; other style books may stipulate that such titles should be in italics. Do not use these marks for names of magazines, newspapers, reference works or the Bible.

"Counterclockwise"

"12 Years a Slave"

But note:

The Oxford English Dictionary

- Use quotation marks for nicknames.

Bob "The Dog" Newland

"Bad Moon Rising" Davis

Hyphen

Whereas the dash creates a break, the *hyphen* is a joiner, a bridge that links words to indicate compound constructions and modifiers. Unfortunately, the hyphen can be as frustrating as it is useful. If you use it to join words that need to work as a unit, and if you use it to avoid confusion, the hyphen will serve you well.

- Use a hyphen to join compound modifiers that precede a noun unless that modifier is preceded by *very* or an *-ly* adverb.

Compound modifiers belong together. They are not part of a series of adjectives and adverbs that can separately describe the word they are modifying. The components of a compound modifier actually modify themselves as they describe the noun:

a fair-weather friend

This is a compound modifier. *Fair* doesn't modify *friend*. It modifies the other modifier, *weather*. Together they modify *friend*. The friend is fair-weathered, not fair and weathered, so we use the hyphen.

a sluggish, unresponsive economy

This is *not* a compound modifier. The economy is both sluggish *and* unresponsive. *Sluggish* doesn't modify *unresponsive*. No hyphen is needed.

If you can insert the conjunction *and* between the modifiers and make sense of the new construction, you do not have a compound modifier. A *sluggish and unresponsive economy* sounds right, but a *fair and weather friend* does not. That should be your signal for a hyphen under this rule, unless the beginning of the compound modifier is *very* or an *-ly* adverb. These words are a clear signal to the reader that a compound modifier is coming, so no hyphen is needed with phrases such as these:

very wealthy philanthropist

warmly received speech

Most compound modifiers are also hyphenated when they follow a form of the linking verb *to be*. In that sense they continue to modify the subject. So, it is proper to write:

Samantha is a well-known anthropologist.

This punctuation is also correct:

Samantha was well-known.

Be sure to make a distinction between a compound modifier and the same words when they are used slightly differently but don't modify anything. It will prevent the improper use of the hyphen:

Last-minute election returns propelled her to victory.

Last-minute modifies *election returns*. Note, however:

He filed for election at the <u>last minute</u>.

Last minute is the object of the preposition *at*. *Last* modifies only *minute*. Be sure to identify all parts of a compound modifier. For example, it's not a *300 year-old* map. It's a *300-year-old* map.

- Use a hyphen for certain prefixes and suffixes.

You'll need to consult a dictionary or stylebook in some cases. There are so many exceptions that you will never guess right all the time! For example, the Associated Press Stylebook stresses that writers hyphenate between the prefix and the following word if the prefix ends in a vowel and the next word begins with the same vowel (for example, *extra-attentive;* exceptions are *cooperate* and *coordinate*). Also hyphenate between the prefix and the following word if that word is capitalized (such as *super-Republican*).

Prefixes that generally take a hyphen include *all-, anti-, ex-, non-* and *pro-*. If you check a dictionary or a stylebook, however, you will find plenty of exceptions.

- Use the hyphen for combinations when the preposition is omitted.

a 98–94 squeaker

the push-me, pull-you dilemma

Apostrophe

The *apostrophe*'s role isn't difficult to demonstrate. In fact, we used it *twice* in the previous sentence. The apostrophe is used to indicate the *possessive case* of nouns and pronouns and to create a *contraction* of two words. Examples:

<u>**Sarah's**</u> **mastery of punctuation is enviable.**
(possessive noun)

<u>**Everyone's**</u> **favorite subject these days is health insurance.**
(possessive pronoun)

<u>**Who's**</u> **going to wake up the professor?**
(contraction for *Who is*)

Nouns as Possessives

We'll focus first on the use of the apostrophe with a variety of nouns, because the placement of the apostrophe and the letter *s* can be confusing.

There are more than a few rules for possessive nouns, but they are not difficult. Here are eight simple ones, consistent with wire service style, for forming possessives of singular and plural nouns.

- If a singular noun does not end in *s*, add *'s*.

the <u>castle's</u> moat

Some guides argue that nouns ending in *ce, x* or *z* (and carrying an *s* or *sh* sound) should have an apostrophe at the end of the word without an *s*. However, it is more common for such words to take an *'s* for simple possession:

the <u>fox's</u> den

Note the exception in the following rule for those possessives that precede a word beginning with *s*:

- If a singular common noun ends in *s*, add *'s* unless the next word begins with *s*. If the next word begins with *s*, add an apostrophe only. (This includes words with *s* and *sh* sounds.)

the <u>boss's</u> evaluation

but:

the <u>boss'</u> swagger

the <u>witness's</u> testimony

but:

the <u>witness'</u> story

but:

for <u>science'</u> sake

- If a singular proper noun ends in *s*, add an apostrophe only.

<u>Davis'</u> defeat

- If a noun is plural in form and ends in *s*, add an apostrophe only, even if the intended meaning of the word (such as mathematics) is singular.

<u>poems'</u> meanings

<u>measles'</u> misery

<u>Marine Corps'</u> spirit

- If a plural noun does not end in *s*, add *'s.*

<u>children's</u> rights

<u>oxen's</u> yoke

<u>media's</u> missteps (*media* is the plural of *medium*)

- If there is joint possession of a noun (both modify the same word), use the correct possessive form for the possessive closest to that noun.

Mutt and <u>Jeff's</u> friendship

her husband and <u>children's</u> trust fund

- If there is separate possession of the same noun, use the correct possessive form for each word.

<u>Billy's</u> and <u>Tom's</u> DVD collections

<u>Zambia's</u> and <u>Paraguay's</u> governments

- In a compound construction, use the correct possessive form for the word closest to the noun.

<u>Society of Friends'</u> gathering

<u>father-in-law's</u> friendship

<u>attorney general's</u> opinion

Other Uses of the Apostrophe

We also use apostrophes to indicate that something has been omitted from a word or a number, as in

I love rock <u>'n'</u> roll. (*'n'* replaces *and*)

I love the music of the <u>'80s.</u> (as in *1980s*)

Here's an interesting use of the apostrophe: to create a plural of a single letter, as in

Tommy got four <u>A's</u> on his report card

However, this rule does not apply with multiple letters, as in

Brenda is going to write a song about the <u>ABCs</u> of love.

Ellipses

We use the *ellipsis mark* (...) to alert the reader that something has been removed from the original or quoted material, that the speaker has hesitated or faltered or that there is more material than is actually cited or used:

> **"We must fight this closure ... we must save this factory."**

The original statement was "We must fight this closure by a management that is bent on saving money with no regard for this town; we must save this factory." In the interest of economy and impact, the writer condensed this statement but preserved its accuracy.

> **Facing the hostile audience, Baker tried to frame his thoughts. "Under these circumstances," he said, "I feel I can no longer serve this community as superintendent. I have tried my best. ... I have always wanted ..." Unable to continue, he left the crowded meeting.**

Note from this example that a period precedes the ellipsis if it ends the sentence. Ellipses should be used sparingly in journalistic writing because they can raise reader suspicion about the importance of the missing phrase and how it affects meaning. Also, too many ellipses can bleed energy away from the content by forcing readers to follow the breaks.

- Other punctuation marks, if needed, come after the quoted material but before the ellipsis.

> **"How would you feel? ..."**

> **"We can't stand for this! ..."**

Parentheses

Two of the most common uses of parentheses (singular is parenthesis) are to signify the addition of needed information and to mark an aside to the main thought.

> *Caveat emptor* **("let the buyer beware") should be every consumer's mantra.**

> **The swimmer deflected any questions about his health. (Some reporters had noted his slight limp.)**

Some other examples:

> **She likes decaffeinated coffee (the cold-water extract type).**

The incumbent refused his opponent's invitation to a debate. (During his last campaign, everyone agreed, he was unprepared for impromptu questions.)

Did you notice the different placement of periods in these examples? Check out the box at the end of this chapter.

A Short Note About Brackets

It's not true that the bracket is a medieval form of the parenthesis. We use brackets (but not often) in these situations:

- To add explanatory material within parentheses.

  He will serve as acting dean (for a three-year period [actually 30 months] starting April 1).

- To add explanatory material or a correction within quoted material.

  Her husband said, "She will teach at Washington State University [the Vancouver campus] when she returns from Iraq."

  The mayor said, "Him [sic] and I go way back and I trust him still."

The term *sic* [from Latin for "thus"] is used to indicate a grammatical or spelling error in quoted material. It is not used frequently these days, but that doesn't mean that errors are disappearing!

Question Mark and Exclamation Point

- If you are asking a direct question, you must use the question mark.

  Why did you sleep through the exam?

- If your question is indirect, no question mark is needed.

  Voters want to know when the bond issue will be on the ballot.

The exclamation point should be used only to express surprise or a strong emotion. In most writing, you probably will employ it only in direct quotation because of the exclamation's sensational nature.

  After receiving his award, the actor said, "I've never been so honored in all my life!"

- Both the question mark and the exclamation point should be included inside quotation marks if the question or exclamation is part of the quoted material.

In direct quotations, remember that the comma is not necessary if the exclamation mark or the question mark is part of the quoted material that precedes attribution:

"Give me a break!" the young man pleaded.

"Do you call this chocolate?" the customer asked.

"Inside or out?" the student asked.
(That's a good question.)

Where do periods, commas, question marks and exclamation marks go when they are used with quotation marks and parentheses?

The period and comma that are part of quoted material *always* go inside the quotation marks. (See below how that may not always apply to a period within parentheses.)

He said, "When I said today, I meant today."

Now, if that quoted material is a question or an exclamation, the same rule applies:

"I said today! Did you think I meant yesterday?"

When to go "outside"? If the question mark or exclamation mark is *not* part of the quoted or parenthetical material, it belongs outside, as in

Have you read the chapter titled "Being Your Own Best Friend"?

A final note, relating to periods and parentheses (and we're not kidding): Look closely at the examples on pp. 101–102, and you'll see that the period is "in or out" depending on what the parenthetical material actually *is*.

Punctuation is more than basic mechanics. Properly employed, punctuation provides clarity, flow, emphasis—even drama. Use punctuation marks wisely and naturally to give your writing the "finish" it deserves.

For additional resources go to **www.cengagebrain.com**

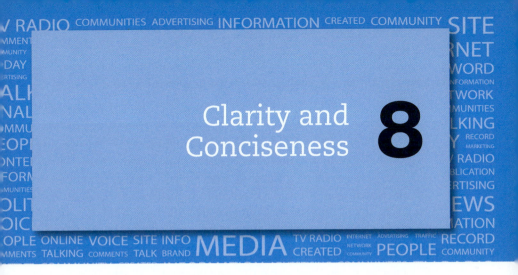
"I was awed at how truly awful language could be on purpose," wrote the proud winner of last year's Bulwer-Lytton Fiction Contest, a whimsical 32-year-old international competition that challenges entrants to compose the worst opening sentence to the worst of all possible novels. Take this one, for example:

> **Cheryl's mind turned like the vanes of a wind-powered turbine, chopping her sparrow-like thoughts into bloody pieces that fell onto a growing pile of forgotten memories.**

Or how about:

> **The dark, drafty old house was lopsided and decrepit, leaning in on itself, the way an aging possum carrying a very heavy, overcooked drumstick in his mouth might list to one side if he were also favoring a torn Achilles tendon, assuming possums have them.**

If you are a word wonk—and what good writer isn't?—you might find yourself on an otherwise gloomy winter afternoon googling "the worst sentence" just for kicks. We did, and the links we found provided hours of lively entertainment. Showcasing truly execrable sentences is apparently a popular sport. We found, in addition to the well-known Bulwer-Lytton Contest, truly awful sentences submitted by economists, physicians, scientific researchers, literary critics and professors of writing who just couldn't resist.

It's fun to read bad writing unless you are (a) its humiliated author or (b) the unfortunate editor who has to fix it. Truly bad writing, not just your run-of-the-mill dull prose, is so blatant in its badness: overwrought, underrealized, meandering, confusing, clunky, sluggish, dense and both downright unreadable and (often) downright laughable. It's also *instructive* to read bad writing. It so obviously shows little respect for language. It so obviously lacks the two qualities essential to successful communication, the very qualities this chapter trumpets: clarity and conciseness.

Let's spend a happy moment with some real stinkers.

"Hmm . . ." thought Abigail as she gazed languidly from the veranda past the bright white patio to the cerulean sea beyond, where dolphins played and seagulls sang, where splashing surf sounded like the tintinnabulation of a thousand tiny bells, where great gray whales bellowed and the sunlight sparkled off the myriad of sequins on the fly fish's bow ties, "time to get my meds checked."

This silly, gloriously verbose sentence was runner-up in the worst sentence contest a few years ago. That writer did it on purpose. Unfortunately, the following writer did not.

The lure of imaginary totality is momentarily frozen before the dialectic of desire hastens on within symbolic chains.

Lest you think that to lack clarity and conciseness prose must be wordy, consider that the sentence you just read is only 18 words. No complicated clauses and phrases. No internal punctuation. Just a "simple" sentence. A simple sentence packed with dense, opaque, impenetrable language and suffocating, tortuous construction. (And yes, we are using fragments on purpose here to make emphatic statements.)

What's common to all these examples is the (near comical) lack of clarity that comes from careless, uncontrolled use of language. What is common, whether it occurs in the 63-word sentence chronicling Abigail's internal monolog or the 18-word "imaginary totality" example, is lack of conciseness, the inability of the writer to communicate keenly, crisply and directly—not to mention sensibly. In this chapter, we'll take a careful look at what it means to write with clarity and conciseness.

Keep in mind that good writing doesn't just happen. Stories don't "write themselves." Skilled writers, talented writers, professional writers work hard at it. They struggle and strain. In fact, contrary to the clichéd admonition, they *do* sweat the small stuff. In fact, it's all about the "small stuff." Clear, concise prose is the result of a series of small, conscious choices that transform the ideas inside writers' heads into the prose we want to read.

Good writers know that direct, powerful writing says *precisely* what the writer means to say—no more, no less, no ambiguity, no blurry meanings, no wasted words, no flabby prose. They ask themselves—they continually, tirelessly ask themselves: *What am I trying to say? Is this what I mean? Is it precisely what I mean? Is this the very best way to say what I mean?* This is the path to clear, forceful prose. You can travel that path, too.

Choosing Words

As we gather our thoughts to begin writing, we are immediately confronted with the most fundamental choice: the individual word. The words we choose must communicate precisely what we mean with a minimum of fuss and a maximum of power. This is particularly true with verbs, the engines of the sentence. Choosing the *correct* verb is a matter of grammar; choosing the *right* verb is a matter of conciseness and clarity. Consider the following word choice problems, remembering that every choice, no matter how minor, no matter how seemingly mechanical, affects the clarity of your prose.

"Verbizing" Nouns

The dying newspaper is committed to <u>monetizing</u> its online presence by <u>componentizing</u> operations and <u>incentivizing</u> its reporters.

The suffix *-ize* is on the loose, "verbizing" and "uglyizing" our language. Some people think you can tack *-ize* onto any noun and create a verb. Most of those makeshift verbs are unnecessary. *Fractionalize*, for example, means nothing more than *split*. Other words with longer linguistic histories, such as *utilize* and *signalize*, actually serve no distinct purpose. *Utilize* has come to mean nothing more than *use*. *Signalize* means signal. Not only are many of these *-ize* words useless, but they are also grating to the ear and uncomfortably bureaucratic.

Of course, yesterday's awkward jargon is today's respectable word. *Pasteurize* must have raised the hackles of 19th-century grammarians, but no one gives it a second thought today. It is difficult to say how many of the newly created, tongue-twisting *-ize* verbs will become permanent additions to our language. (The fewer, the better, we hope.) While we are all awaiting the verdict, we can subject an awkward-sounding *-ize* verb to three tests:

1. Is it listed in the dictionary as an acceptable (not informal, colloquial or slang) word?

2. Does it have a unique meaning?

3. Does it have a sound that is, at the very least, not displeasing?

If the word passes the three tests, use it. If it fails, find another word. Do not "jargonize" and "awkwardize" the language. It may be all right to *pasteurize* milk, but it is not yet acceptable to *chocolatize* it.

Note that nouns sometimes miraculously become verbs (without -izing), like Google, the name of both the search engine and, now, generically, the act of searching for information on the Internet. It's a great word—unique, silly-sounding, unmistakable—and using it both as noun and verb is, well, efficient. It is possible to love words, to honor the language and also to welcome innovation. Clarity, conciseness and grammatical correctness do not equal stodginess.

Vague Words

When we speak, thinking as we talk, sometimes searching for words or fumbling with thoughts, we often insert placeholder phrases like *a type of, a kind of*, or *in terms of*. You might hear yourself say something like: "It was the type of thing I was kind of proud of, I mean in terms of personal accomplishments." You are thinking out loud, speaking before you know what you want to say. Writing is not like that. Writing is thoughtful and premeditated. Think before you write; then edit, edit, edit.

Years of writing term papers and hearing dense and sluggish bureaucratic language—passed along not only by dense and sluggish bureaucrats but also by journalists and, sad to say, textbook authors—have cemented (*cementized?*) in our minds such filler words as *aspect, element, factor, situation, character* and *condition*.

The aspect of the situation that will be a factor will depend on the character of the elements we must contend with.

This is what you say (or write) when you don't know what you're talking about. The result is not only the opposite of clear writing; it is the opposite of *any* communication. Should these words crop up in your prose, weed them out mercilessly.

Euphemisms and "Fancy Words"

The vet doesn't tell you "we're going to have to kill your dog." The vet says, "We're going to have to put Fido to sleep." Putting an animal "to sleep" is a euphemism, an expression designed to be less offensive or disturbing than the word or phrase it replaces. Most of us who visit the "powder room" are not there to apply powder. We are there to use the toilet. "Powder room" is a euphemism. Those who frequent a "gentlemen's club" are not going for the purpose of sitting in leather club chairs, sipping brandy and discussing the finer points of horse breeding. They are there to stare at naked women. "Gentlemen's club" is a euphemism for a strip club.

Euphemisms are all around us. The term used for radiation leaked from an improperly operating nuclear power plant—a mightily disturbing event—is the lovely phrase "sunshine units." The military wins the dubious prize for creating both the most—and the most chilling—euphemisms.

Enhanced interrogation techniques is the military's term for what is widely considered torture. *Entry into a nonpermissive environment* is the military's way of evading the word *invasion*. *Friendly fire* softens the terrible tragedy of the action it describes: gunfire against troops by their own troops. *Collateral damage* is a euphemism for killing civilians. *Police action* is an undeclared war. *Pacification* is coercive force, including warfare. Euphemisms like this, sometimes called "doublespeak," can be a way of shielding the bearer of negative information from taking responsibility for the information or a way of shielding the recipients of the information from its true horrors.

When HSBC fired nearly 1,000 people last year, the mega-bank announced it would be "demising the roles of nearly 1,000 employees"—*demising the roles?*—a "new low" in the language of lay-offs, according to an article in "The New York Times." Writers can't stop others from manufacturing euphemisms, but they can refuse to transmit them.

A related clarity problem is "fancy words." We don't mean three-dollar words like *prestidigitation* or *ovolactovegetarianism.* We mean silly, inflated words that take the place of good, plain, ordinary, serviceable words: *disambiguate* for clarify, to cite one particularly egregious example. Beware of more common inflated words like *facility* for building, *infrastructure* for roads and bridges, *domicile* for home. Stay clear of these pretensions. If others use them, your responsibility as a public communicator is to *not* pass them on.

> "Poor Faulkner. Does he really think big emotions come from big words?"
> —Ernest Hemingway

Jargon

Poker players talk about a "bellybuster"—an inside straight draw. Computer geeks refer to problems caused by the incompetence of users as "PEBKACs," which stands for "Problem exists between keyboard and chair." Cops might say "the skell got three hots and a cot" instead of the felon was sentenced to jail. This is jargon, the specialized language of a group of people engaged in an activity, trade or occupation.

Jargon is shorthand communication, a kind of code. It works well within the group because everyone knows and understands it. Sometimes jargon migrates and becomes part of accepted and understood vocabulary. Spam, meaning unsolicited email (not the yummy canned meat-like product), is a good example. But jargon is often confusing to others. A secret language, it can act to insulate the group and exclude nonmembers from the conversation.

Because media writers have a responsibility to communicate clearly and simply to wider audiences, we should be jargon slayers not jargon purveyors.

Here is a researcher deep in the throes of jargon:

Within this regional population, total caloric intake from all sources regardless of nutritional value as measured by standard methods is insufficient to balance overall metabolic output, including both resting and active components.

(Translation: These people don't have enough food.)

Jargon can be used to obscure ideas or make ordinary ideas sound more important. It can also be used to hide meaning or desensitize people to issues. For a writer to perpetuate such jargon signals a failure to communicate. Using jargon does not make you sound impressive. On the contrary, you impress (and help) your audience by lucidly explaining difficult material, not repeating words and phrases you do not understand.

Redundancy and Wordiness

In the world of writing, less is often more: the economical phrase, the lean sentence, the stark image. Such writing grabs readers and stays with them. On the other hand, clutter—words that serve no purpose—interfere with clear and memorable communication.

Make your words count. Ignorance of the real meanings of words, attempts at false erudition, repetition of other people's jargon, murky thinking and sheer sloppiness can all result in prose that is wordy or redundant. Consider these all-too-common examples of redundancy:

basic fundamentals
(Fundamentals *are*, by definition, the basics.)

absolutely certain
(as opposed to slightly uncertain certain?)

actual experience
(An experience is something that *actually* occurred.)

mutual cooperation
(*Cooperation* means "acting for mutual benefit." *Mutual* is redundant.)

end result
(*Result*, by definition, is the consequence.)

advance warning
(A warning does, by definition, tell you in advance.)

incumbent officeholder
(The definition of *incumbent* is "officeholder.")

consensus of opinion
(*Consensus* means "collective opinion.")

repeat again
(*Repeat* includes "again" in its definition.)

refer back
(*Refer* includes "back" in its definition.)

completely destroyed
(Destruction is complete.)

Also note *added bonus, anonymous stranger* (as opposed to all those familiar strangers), *ATM machine* (what do you think the "M" stands for?), *armed gunman.*

> "The most valuable of all talents is that of never using two words when one will do."
>
> —Thomas Jefferson

A number of wordy, sluggish expressions have crept into writing. Here are some of the more common ones to avoid:

Instead of	Use
as of now	now
at the conclusion of	after
at the present time	now
at this point in time	now
concerning the matter of	about
despite the fact that	although
due to the fact that	because
on account of	because
seeing as how	because
during the course of	during
there is a chance that	may/might/could
while at the same time	while

Just *One* Word

Flabby prose is the enemy of clarity and conciseness. Sometimes that flabbiness is easy to see—verbose sentences, unintelligible jargon—but sometimes it is subtler. It may come in the form of a single unnecessary word. Should you care about a single unnecessary word? You bet. Here are two you will want to eschew.

Avoiding *up*

She was selected to <u>head up</u> the commission.

The candidate must <u>face up</u> to the issues.

The storm <u>slowed up</u> [down] traffic all morning.

None of these verbs needs the preposition *up*. *Up* doesn't add meaning to these verbs; it takes away crispness. This may seem like a minor point, but it is at this basic level that good writing begins.

She was selected to <u>head</u> the commission.

The candidate must <u>face</u> the issues.

The storm <u>slowed</u> traffic all morning.

Beware of *free up* (free), *wake up* (awake), *stand up* (stand) and *shake up* (shake). In these instances *up* is more than unnecessary; it is sloppy.

Of course some verbs need *up* to complete their meaning. *Make* does not mean the same thing as *make up*. *Break* is not synonymous with *break up*. *Up* is necessary for the meaning of *pick up*. In these cases *up* is not clutter, but neither is it strong, precise writing.

The editor accused the reporter of <u>making up</u> sources.
(weak)

The editor accused the reporter of <u>fabricating</u> sources.
(stronger)

The investigation <u>broke up</u> the crime syndicate.
(weak)

The investigation <u>shattered</u> the crime syndicate.
(stronger)

The market for narrative nonfiction is <u>picking up</u>.
(weak)

The market for narrative nonfiction is <u>improving</u>.
(stronger)

That

That performs several grammatical functions. It is an adjective:

<u>That</u> book changed my life.
(*That* describes book.)

It is a demonstrative pronoun:

That will change your life.
(*That* takes the place of a noun.)

It is a relative pronoun:

This is a book that will change your life.
(*That* introduces a relative clause.)

It is a conjunction:

The author said that writing the book changed her life.
(*That* links two independent clauses.)

The troublesome uses of *that* are as a conjunction and as a relative pronoun. Simply put, writers overuse the word. *That* is often unnecessary in a sentence. Its inclusion can rob the sentence of its grace and rhythm. If a word does not add meaning, get rid of it. Consider these sentences, all of which would be crisper without *that:*

The author said that writing the book changed her life.

The researchers admitted that they falsified data.

Government sources say that the study is flawed.

Often all you need do is remove the useless *that*; however, some sentences demand revision. Conciseness is the issue:

This is a book that will change your life.
(wordy)

This book will change your life.
(improved)

Police recovered the laptop that was stolen.
(wordy)

Police recovered the stolen laptop.
(improved)

That is sometimes used legitimately to link sentence parts. To discover whether *that* is necessary to a sentence, ask yourself two questions:

1. Can *that* be eliminated with no change in the meaning of the sentence?

2. Can the clause introduced by *that* be expressed more succinctly?

If you answer *yes* to either question, edit or rewrite.

> "Clutter is the disease of American writing. We are a society strangling in unnecessary words, circular constructions, pompous frills and meaningless jargon."
> —William Zinsser, "On Writing Well: The Classic Guide to Writing Nonfiction"

The "inclusive" *man*, the "generic" *he*

Let's talk clarity here, not ideology.

We understand the word *man* to mean a male human being (as in "The man wore a suit and tie"). But we often use the same word to mean both male and female human beings (as in "Peace on earth, goodwill to *men*" or "All *men* are created equal"). How can one word simultaneously support two different meanings? How can one word be both gender-exclusive (male only) and gender-inclusive (male and female)? It's like saying: "Sometimes when I write the word *apple*, I mean apple. But other times when I write the word *apple*, I mean apple and orange. I leave it to you to figure out which is the operative meaning." It's confusing. It makes for unclear prose and muddied meaning.

When elementary school girls and boys were asked to draw pictures to accompany a hypothetical history textbook with supposedly gender-inclusive chapter titles like "Colonial Man" and "Democratic Man"—*man* here was supposed to be synonymous with *people*—they weren't confused at all: All the boys and just about all the girls drew pictures of men—male human beings, that is. We may talk about the gender-inclusive *man*, but in fact *man* is generally understood as male only.

If you mean "male only," then, of course, use *man*. If you mean both men and women, our language has a wide variety of inclusive words that promote clarity. General references should always be inclusive:

Instead of	Use
man, men	person, people
mankind	people
founding fathers	founders, forebears
gentlemen's agreement	informal agreement
manpower	workforce
to man (verb)	to staff, operate

Note that many words with *man* in them have nothing to do with gender. The root *man*, from Latin and then French, means *hand*, giving us words like *man*ual, *man*ufacturing and *man*ipulate.

Just as *man* cannot mean both men only and men and women both, so too *he* cannot refer to a male person at certain times and both genders at other times. *He* is not generic. It is specific. When you use *he*, you communicate maleness, whether that is your intention or that is the reality. For example:

A doctor must care first about <u>his</u> patients.

A child will gain confidence if <u>he</u> is allowed to make <u>his</u> own decisions.

Are all doctors men? Are all children male? Use of *he* or *him* presumes and communicates gender exclusivity. The clarity rule is simple: Never use *he* or *him* unless you are referring to a male. If you mean to be gender-inclusive, you have three choices:

1. When you must use a pronoun to refer to a noun of undetermined or inclusive gender *doctor, child*), recast the sentence with plurals. *They* and *them* are gender-inclusive:

   <u>Doctors</u> must care first about <u>their</u> patients.

   <u>Children</u> will gain confidence if <u>they</u> are allowed to make their <u>own</u> decisions.

2. If sentence structure or meaning would be impaired by the plural, use *he or she, his or her,* or *him or her.* This construction can be a bit awkward— but not as awkward as excluding more than half the human race:

   A doctor must care first about <u>his or her</u> patients.

3. Consider whether the pronoun is actually needed. Perhaps the sentence can be rewritten:

   A child will gain confidence if allowed to make independent decisions.

The words *everyone* and *everybody* can present grammatical problems here. Their meaning is clearly plural, as in *many people* (presumably both male and female). But grammatically, these words take the singular, as in *Everyone* is *invited to the party.* Because they take the singular but imply the plural, look what can happen:

Everyone should remain in *his* seat.

To be grammatically correct, the sentence needs a singular pronoun. But a singular pronoun—*he* is almost always chosen, not *she*—communicates gender exclusivity. What to do? First, what *not* to do: Do not break a grammatical rule to create gender inclusivity. Do *not* write:

Everyone should remain in *their* seat.

You could write:

Everyone should remain in *his* or *her* seat,

but there's a clunkiness factor at work here. Better to find another way to say *everybody*, as in:

People should remain in their seats.

All concertgoers should remain in their seats.

Putting Words Together

Clear, concise, coherent writing depends on more than careful word choice. Proper placement of words is imperative. Misplacement mistakes can easily harm the clarity of your prose.

Misplaced Words

In a sentence, a modifier needs to point directly and clearly to what it modifies. This means placing the modifier next to or as close as possible to what it is modifying. Adverbs like *only, nearly, almost, just, scarcely, even, hardly* and *merely* create the biggest potential difficulty because their placement can drastically change the meaning of the sentence. Note how placement changes meaning in the following examples:

<u>Only</u> he can help you.
(No one else can help you.)

He can <u>only</u> help you.
(He can't do anything more than help you.)

He can help <u>only</u> you.
(He can't help anyone else.)

Notice how the placement of *almost* in the next two sentences changes the meaning:

Negotiations <u>almost</u> broke down on every clause in the contract.
(Negotiations did not quite break down.)

Negotiations broke down on <u>almost</u> every clause in the contract.
(Just about every clause caused problems during negotiations.)

When we speak we often have a devil-may-care attitude toward the placement of adverbs. But because placement most surely changes meaning, stick to the old rule: Place the adverb (or other word) next to or as close as possible to the word you intend it to modify.

Misplaced/Dangling Phrases and Clauses

Like individual words, phrases and clauses should be placed next to or near what they modify. Sometimes the effect of a misplaced phrase is (unintentionally) hilarious, as in this gem:

> **Approximately the size of a piece of paper, Apple claims that the iPad is the most intuitive way to experience the web.**

Apple is the largest publicly traded company in the United States, with more than $440 billion in shares. It employs 70,000-plus people and maintains more than 400 retail stores in fourteen countries, as well as the online Apple Store and iTunes Store, the latter of which is the world's largest music retailer. In other words, it is quite a bit bigger than a piece of paper. That's right: When the proper noun *Apple* appears immediately following the phrase *approximately the size of a piece of paper*, the phrase modifies that noun. Here's another one:

> **To learn the craft of writing, discipline is needed.**

As constructed, the phrase *to learn the craft of writing* modifies the word *discipline*, but that makes no sense. The sentence needs to be revised:

> **To learn the craft of writing, you must be disciplined.**

Consider how placement changes meaning—and can cause confusion.

> **The proposal that the student council is debating will alter the university's free speech policy.**

> **The proposal will alter the university's free speech policy that the student council is debating.**

In the first sentence, the student council's *proposal* is being debated. In the second example, the university's *policy* is being debated. What did the writer mean?

Split Constructions

Just as modifiers need to rest closely to what they modify, so other parts of the sentence must be placed carefully to maintain clarity and coherence of thought.

Split verbs often lead to incoherence. In most cases it is best to keep auxiliary verbs next to the main verb and to avoid splitting infinitives. Consider what happens to sentence unity and graceful expression when you separate auxiliary verbs from the main verb:

> **She <u>has</u> for the entire spring semester <u>subsisted</u> on RockStar and Kale Krunch.**
> (auxiliary and main verb split)

> **For the entire spring semester, she <u>has subsisted</u> on RockStar and Kale Krunch.**

The more words you place between the verb parts, the less coherent the sentence becomes. Occasionally, however, it is acceptable—even preferable—to split a multipart verb. Almost always the verb is split by a single word, an adverb:

> **Junk food <u>has</u> always <u>been</u> an issue in the school cafeteria.**

Placing *always* between the verb parts does not hinder coherence. In fact, it adds emphasis.

Infinitives (*to* forms of the verb) should also, in most cases, remain intact. Split infinitives contribute to awkwardness and interfere with coherent expression. A sentence should read smoothly and make sense:

> **The parent group promised <u>to</u> within the next month <u>explore</u> the feasibility of a school-community vegetable garden.**
> (split infinitive)

> **The parent group promised <u>to</u> <u>explore</u> the feasibility of a school-community vegetable garden within the next month.**
> (improved)

To aid sentence clarity and help readers or listeners understand quickly what you are trying to say, keep the subject and the verb as close as possible. Look what happens to coherence when subject and verb are interrupted by lengthy explanatory material:

> **The school <u>board</u>, after months of rancorous public debate resulting in**
> (subj.)
>
> **the cancellation of all vending machine contracts, <u>endorsed</u> the**
> (verb)
>
> **garden proposal.**

The sentence forces readers or listeners to wade through 16 words between the subject (*board*) and its verb (*endorsed*). But readers may have neither the time nor the inclination to slog through such constructions, and listeners can easily lose the thread of meaning. Be kind to your audience. Keep subject and verb close:

> **After months of rancorous public debate resulting in the cancellation of all vending machine contracts, the <u>board endorsed</u> the garden proposal.**

Consider one more common splitting problem: a verb and its complements. The simplest construction to understand is subject–verb–object. It answers the basic question: *Who did what to whom?* Just as splitting the subject (*who*) from the verb (*did what*) interferes with clarity and coherence, so too does splitting the verb (*did what*) from its complement (*to whom*). Keep the verb and its complements (object, adverb, descriptive phrase) as close together as possible. You will promote sentence unity, readability and coherence. Consider this example:

> **Consumer advocates <u>protested</u> yesterday morning in front of three**
> (verb)
>
> **local toy stores <u>what they say is the marketing of violence to children</u>**
> (complement)
>
> **<u>through the sale of toy guns.</u>**

This sentence is clumsy. To avoid losing coherent thought—and your audience—rewrite:

> **Consumer advocates protested today what they say is the marketing of violence to children through the sale of toy guns. Marching [picketing, assembling, gathering] in front of three local toy stores, they ...**

Making Sense

Every good grammatical decision you make contributes to clarity, conciseness and coherence. Choosing strong, precise words is the first step. Placing these words correctly is the next. Focusing on the architecture of sentences is the third level.

Passive Voice

Here's a quiz for you: Would you rather have someone call your writing (a) crisp, clear, lively, agile and spirited or (b) confusing, listless, stagnant and leaden? If you chose (a), read on. If you chose (b), well, we know you were just kidding. . . .

The adjectives in (a) describe *active* writing, which can mean many things. For the purposes of this discussion, we are referring to *active voice*. The adjectives in (b) characterize *passive* writing—or *passive voice*—one of the enemies of clear and concise prose.

You will remember that we introduced passive voice in Chapter 3 (p. 33). To review: *Voice* refers to the form of the verb. The subject acts when you use the *active voice* verb form. In the *passive voice*, the person or thing performing the action becomes instead the object of the sentence; it does not act, but is acted *upon* by the verb. Passive voice is *not* the path to crisp, clear writing. Here's why:

1. **Passive voice can make a sentence unnecessarily awkward and wordy** by reversing the expected relationship of who did what to whom. Subject–verb–object is almost always the clearest, smoothest construction. It is also the most succinct. Changing the order means adding unnecessary words:

   Investigations are being conducted by the attorney general's office into the financial irregularities.
   (passive)

   The attorney general is investigating the financial irregularities.
   (active)

2. **Passive voice creates false formality**, making a sentence sound impersonal, bureaucratic and overinflated.

   It has been revealed by company insiders that "creative accounting" and bookkeeping irregularities are part of a larger pattern of corporate misbehavior.
   (passive, unnecessarily formal)

   Company insiders revealed that "creative accounting" and bookkeeping irregularities are part of a larger pattern of corporate misbehavior.
   (active)

   "Creative accounting" and bookkeeping irregularities are part of a larger pattern of corporate malfeasance, according to company insiders.
   (active)

The tendency to use passive voice to create formality may come from term paper writing or textbook reading, where such dense and stilted sentences often reside. As a favorite construction of politicians and scientists, passive voice is all around us, but as writers we must strive to communicate simply and directly. To refresh your memory about how to recognize and correct passive voice, see p. 35.

Note that occasionally an expert writer might use passive voice as a stylistic device to create a sense of detachment, a sense that no one is taking responsibility for certain actions, a feeling that actions are out of control or mysterious. Purposefully obscuring or removing prominence from the doer might create suspense. Passive voice can be a stylistic element.

Parallel Structure

Parallel structure aligns related ideas and presents them through the repetition of grammatical structure. It is vital to both clarity and unity, and helps create rhythm and grace in a sentence. Simple. Now, prepare to cringe. What follows is a severely grammatically challenged sentence that, among other things, lacks parallel structure. The *real* cringe part? The sentence is the catalog copy for a class on ... writing.

This class is designed to assist students not only in writing their novel but to get it published.

The ideas that need to be expressed in parallel form (*and aren't*) are the two stated goals of the class: to help students write their novels, to help students get their novels published. (Note that these are now expressed in parallel grammatical forms.) We might also mention that *not only* always needs to be paired with *but also* to set up parallelism—which does not happen in this sentence. And we'd be remiss if we did not mention (although this is not a parallelism issue) that thoughtless sentence construction makes it appear that *all* the students in the class will be writing *one* novel.

Let's look at sentences that are constructed with parallel structure.

To create parallel structure using single words, you use a series of words that are the same part of speech. For example:

The scheme was complicated, clever and illegal.

The related ideas are the characterizations of the scheme. The grammatical pattern is the repetition of single adjectives.

To create parallel structure using phrases or clauses, replicate the grammatical pattern:

Exercise can <u>clear the mind</u>, <u>energize the body</u> and <u>lift the spirits</u>.
(repeating phrases)

Because we have the resources, because we know what's right and because we have no other choice, we should rid our air and water of toxic chemicals.
(repeating clauses)

Parallel structure binds ideas and enhances the audience's understanding of each idea by creating a lucid, easily recognizable pattern. If you begin a sentence by establishing a particular grammatical pattern and then break it, you create confusion and disharmony.

Parallel structure is commonly used to introduce complementary, contrasting or sequential ideas. The relationship between the ideas can be implicit (as in the examples offered thus far) or it can be made apparent by using signal words:

- Complementary relationship: *both/and, not only/but also.*

- Contrasting relationship: *either/or, neither/nor.*

- Sequential relationship: *first/second/third.*

   Both the addition of attic insulation and the installation of triple-paned windows will dramatically lower energy costs.
   (complementary relationship, parallel structure)

   Either we solve the problem or we suffer the consequences.
   (contrasting relationship, parallel structure)

   First, define the problem; second, gather the information; third, brainstorm the alternatives.
   (sequential relationship, parallel structure)

Whether you make the relationship explicit by using signal words or implicit by letting the ideas speak for themselves, parallel structure is vital to clarity and coherence.

Sentence Fragments

As you remember from Chapter 3, a *fragment* is a group of words that lacks a subject, a predicate, a complete thought or any combination of the three. Grammatically, a fragment cannot stand alone. When readers see a group of words beginning with a capital letter and ending with a period, they expect a complete sentence. If instead you offer them a fragment, you confuse them. Unintentional fragments hinder both coherence and clarity.

   Bloggers have revolutionized international reporting. Although there are credibility issues. Traditional media are citing blogs as sources.

This fragment (underlined) is confusing. Do the credibility issues reside with the bloggers or with the traditional media? Maybe the writer meant:

   Although there are credibility issues, bloggers are revolutionizing international reporting.

But it may be that the writer meant:

Although there are credibility issues, traditional media are using blogs as sources.

Fragments leave your audience hanging, forcing them to guess your intended meaning. Offer clear, complete thoughts. Fragments used knowingly, sparingly and stylistically are another story. See Chapter 9 for a more in-depth discussion on fragments as style.

Run-On Sentences

A *run-on sentence* is composed of two, three or any number of whole, complete sentences joined together ungrammatically. Chapters 3 and 7 discussed the run-on as a grammatical problem. Here we want to emphasize it as an obstacle to concise and coherent writing.

The two most common run-on sentences are those inappropriately linked with *and* and those incorrectly spliced with commas. Both can confuse and frustrate a reader:

The public schools must deal with a shrinking budget and class sizes will increase.
(run-on)

When you use *and* to link two independent clauses as above, you are saying that the two thoughts reinforce or directly complement each other or follow one another sequentially. If this isn't the case, as in the preceding example, you have created not just a run-on but also a less-than-coherent sentence. If the thoughts in the clauses are not related in a definable, explicit way, rewrite the run-on as two separate sentences. If the thoughts are related, use a connecting word to signal the correct relationship:

Because the public schools must deal with a shrinking budget, class sizes will increase.
(improved)

Note that the run-on was corrected by subordinating one thought (clause) to another to clarify and make explicit the relationship between the two clauses.

Commas alone cannot link independent clauses. Independent clauses are sentences all on their own. To link them grammatically, you have a number of choices. Consider this run-on:

The legislature mandated cutbacks throughout the public school system, class sizes increased dramatically, elective classes decreased significantly, teachers were instructed to take three furlough days.

Here's one grammatical fix:

> **The legislature mandated cutbacks throughout the public school system, including increased class size, decreased elective classes and three furlough days for teachers.**

Or depending on intended meaning, you could subordinate one independent clause to the others.

> **<u>Soon after</u> the legislature mandated cutbacks throughout the public school system, class size increased dramatically, elective classes decreased significantly, and teachers were asked to take three furlough days.**

Clarity, Conciseness, Coherence

Writers write to be understood. Whether they are writing to inform, amuse, uplift, persuade or cajole, their thoughts must be clear; their sentences must be comprehensible. Clarity, conciseness and coherence begin with individual word choice. From that point every grammatical decision either enhances or detracts from this triple goal. Imprecision, clutter, misplaced phrases and murky construction have no place in good writing. The goal is lean, powerful communication.

For additional resources go to **www.cengagebrain.com**

Open your eyes! Stylish prose is everywhere:

... in this *how-can-you-not-read-on* paragraph that begins an award-winning story in "GQ":

Last fall, one of Spain's greatest matadors took a horn to the face. It was a brutal goring, among the most horrific in the history of bullfighting. Miraculously, Juan Jose Padilla was back in the bullring— sí, fighting bulls—a mere five months later. And in the process of losing half his sight, he somehow managed to double his vision.

... in this clever lyric from Jay-Z:

I'm not just a businessman. I am a business, man.

... in this witty blog post:

My daughter drives.

Are there three scarier, more exciting words in the English language? Three words that simultaneously hold such promise and such peril, that signal such joy, fear, expectation, liberation—and expense?

... in this wallop of a sentence created for the American Lung Association:

If you want more information about lung cancer, keep smoking.

... or, on a much lighter note, in these clever ads for Starburst candies:

Tropical. But thoroughly enjoyed by pale people who burn easily. It's a pack of contradictions.

The islands are calling. Yet the islands couldn't possibly know your cell number. It's a pack of contradictions.

Style makes reading a pleasure. It gives power and punch to storytelling in all its forms. Style makes what you have to say memorable. It is an ever-escalating, lifelong and—you'll have to trust us on this—joyful challenge faced every day by writers who care deeply about their work and their readers. Is that you? We hope so.

Style comes from the Latin word *stylus*, "a pointed instrument used for writing." Few of us use pointed instruments to write anymore (unless the tips of acrylic nails tapping on a tablet count), but style could still be defined, metaphorically if not literally, as "a pointed instrument used for writing."

What is Style?

Style is the writer's unique vision—and the lively, original expression of that vision—that transforms text from interesting to irresistible, from noticeable to unforgettable. Style is first and foremost the reflection of the writer's way of seeing and thinking, and so decisions about style begin with the kind of story a writer decides to pursue and how the writer approaches and thinks about the material. Style has much to do how the writer approaches the story, and with the depth, breath, originality and quirkiness of the writer's research.

Style is a way of seeing. Take, for example, this description of two brothers in a Tad Friend piece in "The New Yorker." The language couldn't be plainer. The sentence construction couldn't be more utilitarian. The style—and this excerpt has it—comes from the quirky way the author sees his subjects.

> **Matt, who is forty-three, is tall, bearded and chiseled, and he wears interesting glasses. His brother, thirty-four, has an identical beard but is shorter and portlier and less groomed, as if a sculptor started carving a copy of Matt and then lost interest.**

> "It isn't enough to have smooth and pretty language. You have to surprise the reader ... Provoke the reader. Astonish the reader. Writing that has no surprises is as bland as oatmeal."
>
> —Anne Bernays

Of course, style is evident in the writing itself—although often not obvious. Is there talent involved? You bet. But style is also the product of purposeful choices, the culmination of many small things done well, the result of sheer hard work. Style has an important place in *all* writing—from a lengthy feature piece to the one-sentence captions under a multimedia slide show; from the script for a documentary to the tweet you want everyone to read.

Novice writers, and some experienced ones as well, often don't have the right idea about style.

- They believe if they write clean, uncluttered prose, their writing will lack style.

- They believe style is like a garnish or a spicy condiment added after the fact to bring zest to bland writing.

- They believe style is always flashy.

- They fear that style, because it is hard to define ("I don't know what it is, but I know it when I see it"), is therefore mysterious and unattainable.

Oh boy, are they are *wrong.*

Style emerges from—and cannot exist without—crisp, clean language use. First come the fundamentals: strong verbs, grammatical consistency, well-constructed sentences. Then comes style. Novelist John Updike looks at style by comparing the process of writing to the process of becoming a musician. Musicians begin by learning to identify and play individual notes. They learn how to read music. They practice scales. They play simple compositions. Only after mastering these fundamentals can they begin to develop their own manner of musical expression, their own style. Writers too must master the basics before they can find their own voice.

Style, then, has little to do with ostentatious language. Window dressing (a gaggle of adjectives, for example), verbal ornamentation (big words or purple prose) and fancy tricks do not generally contribute to compelling writing. In fact, verbal flashiness can obscure coherent thought. There is nothing flashy about this sentence:

This year Americans will consume 35 million cows, 115 million pigs and nine billion birds.

In choosing to express meat as animals—cows instead of beef, pigs instead of pork—the writer takes us by surprise and makes us think about our consumption in a different way. These simple word choices create a powerful sentence that does more than communicate information.

The final misconception, that style is mysterious and unattainable, is the hardest to discount. Because it is unique to the individual writer, style does seem to defy definition. But that doesn't mean it's mysterious. It means it's personal, idiosyncratic and distinctive. Far from being enigmatic, style is the sum of a series of good, solid decisions—many of them as basic as word choice or sentence construction—that a writer is aware enough, and smart and experienced enough, to make time after time.

As we've said, style begins with a unique vision—and this cannot be taught. What can be taught (or at least learned) is how to give expression to that vision. The process is rooted in correctness and clarity, and then purposefully, creatively, energetically moves to something more: stylish, graceful, compelling writing. This is not an easy task. It is, after all, a writer's life work, the evolution of craft. Style doesn't just happen. It is thoughtfully, patiently learned.

Let's demystify style by examining some of its key components: liveliness, originality, rhythm and sound and imagery.

Liveliness

Lively writing is not excitable, overwrought, exclamation mark-studded prose, but uncluttered composition that moves along at a good clip, involving readers or listeners and carrying them briskly from paragraph to paragraph. Like all components of style, liveliness depends not only on the way you use the language but also on what you have to say.

Style and substance go hand in hand. Your skills as a keen observer, active listener, thoughtful interviewer and thorough information gatherer net the raw material. Your skill as a writer transforms that material into vibrant prose. Here's how to make your writing lively.

Choose Verbs Carefully

Strong, precise verbs give energy to a sentence; weak, vague or over-modified verbs sap a sentence of its power. Instead of tacking on adverbs to clarify the meaning of a verb, spend time searching for the one right word.

Instead of	Use
talk incessantly	jabber, chatter, blab
look into deeply	delve, probe, plumb
walk slowly	amble, trudge, saunter
eat quickly	gobble, wolf

> "The road to hell is paved with adverbs."
> —Stephen King, "On Writing: A Memoir of the Craft"

Consider the lively litany of verbs in this explanation of the immersion research a writer put herself through to gather material for a book:

I've been dunked, pinched, punctured, lasered, biopsied, scanned, meridianed and Reiki-ed. I've been injected, inspected (rejected), assayed, assessed, rated (and berated).

Use Intensifiers Sparingly

The adverbs *very, really, truly, completely, extremely, positively, absolutely, awfully* and *so* that *so very* often (see what we mean?) sprinkle our casual conversation often add nothing but clutter to written work. They show sloppiness of thought and generally add a too colloquial tone to writing. Instead of intensifying a weak word, search for a strong, precise one.

Instead of	Use
very angry	irate
extremely tired	exhausted
really happy	elated
awfully hot	scorching

"Don't say you were a bit confused and sort of tired ... Be tired. Be confused ... Don't hedge your prose with little timidities. Good writing is lean and confident."

—William Zinsser

When you've found a strong word, leave it alone. Don't rob it of its impact by unnecessarily intensifying it:

~~really~~ famished
~~extremely~~ sweltering
~~truly~~ extravagant

Avoid Redundancies

Understand the meanings of words before you use them. *More equal, more parallel* and *most unique* are redundant expressions you can easily avoid if you pay attention to the meanings of *equal, parallel* and *unique*.

Edit to Remove Wordiness

Nothing destroys the vitality of prose faster, or as completely, as does verbosity, clutter, "purple prose," or bureaucratese. Each word, each phrase, each clause, each sentence should survive your rigorous editing process because it adds meaning, substance or color to the piece. Making every word count is the challenge. You may want to review what we've said about "Vague Words," "Euphemisms and 'Fancy Words'" and "Jargon" in Chapter 8.

Use Active Voice

As you know, active voice contributes to clear, vigorous sentence construction. In an active-voice sentence, the actor performs the action. In a passive-voice sentence, the actor has the action performed upon it. Passive-voice construction almost always weakens the verb and adds unnecessary words. It often sounds stilted and formal.

That's the rule. But style is sometimes about breaking rules. The following example illustrates purposeful—we think masterful—use of passive voice as an element of style. Note how the formality of passive voice creates a tongue-in-cheek contrast between the stilted treatment of the subject and the not-so-serious subject itself:

> **Condemnations have been made. Mildly menacing Internet comments have been exchanged. A lawsuit and a police report have been filed. Multitudes of parking altercations have occurred, with government officials summoned.**
>
> **Yes, frozen yogurt is back.**

Use Present Tense

Present tense often allows the reader or listener to experience the story as it unfolds. When you use present tense as an element of style, you create a scene with urgency and immediacy. Consider this account, written in present tense, from a longer piece about a women's basketball team:

> **Down near the basket, Karen is guarding Courtney, a five-foot-two freshman walk-on. Courtney has the ball. Karen is trying hard to get into the rhythm of this fast-paced drill. Courtney is little and quick, but Karen is quick too.**
>
> **She lunges at Courtney, looking to steal the ball. At the same time, Courtney moves toward Karen. Karen's right hand connects with Courtney's shoulder. The fingers jam back. Karen hears a pop. For a moment, the sound makes her so nauseous that she doesn't feel the pain. Then she feels the pain. She freezes in place, feet planted on the floor, white-faced, disoriented. She grabs her hand. It is her shooting hand.**

Of course, the scene took place in the past. The writer is recounting it for the audience much later. But the present tense makes us feel as if we are there watching. The scene is alive. Not all stories can or should be told in present tense. Often past or future tenses are essential for historical accuracy. But the technique of narrowing the gap between audience and story by using present tense has many applications. Scene setting is certainly one of them.

Another is *attribution*. Using present tense to attribute quotations or present dialog in a story—*says* instead of *said*, for example—shows the immediacy and current relevance of the comments. If a person said something yesterday, he or she would be likely to say the same thing today (unless, of course, we're talking about politicians or disgraced sports heroes). Present tense attribution, like present tense in general, subtly quickens the pace of the story.

No single element ensures lively writing. But if you use strong, precise language; rid your prose of clutter; stick with the active voice and use, where appropriate, the present tense, your writing will be crisper, snappier and more inviting.

Originality

Originality of style cannot be separated from originality of substance. If, as a thinker, observer, interviewer and cultural forager, you gather fresh material and come to novel insights, the written work you produce can be distinctive and original. When magazine writer Mary Roach visited Florida to write about, of all things, Tupperware, she began her story this way:

> **The Tupperware World Headquarters in Orlando, Florida, is a collection of long, low modular buildings, the sort of shapes you could easily stack one on top of another for just-right storage in your pantry, fridge or freezer, if that's the sort of person you were.**

The playful tone and the unique visual image create an unusually enticing first sentence. This is what originality is all about: a novel vision translated into simple but imaginative language. This is style.

Avoid clichés (like the plague)

A *cliché*, by definition, lacks originality. It is a trite or overused expression or idea. It's the image or the phrase that springs immediately to mind. We've heard it before; we've read it before. We know it *like the back of our hand*. It's as *comfortable as an old shoe*. Get it? A cliché is someone else's idea, and the more it is used, the less power it has. As poet and author Donald Hall writes, "When we put words together ... we begin to show our original selves, or we show a dull copy of someone else's original." Note the following cliché-ridden remark from an economist offering the year's forecast.

Let's remember we climbed up the hill pretty darned quickly. We've had the rug pulled out from under us, but we've picked ourselves up, and maybe we can see the light at the end of the tunnel.

If the *light at the end of the tunnel* serves only to illuminate a cliché, it's not worth the trip, is it? The challenge is to use your imaginative and linguistic powers to create original expressions.

Because we can't resist, here's a gloriously awful example of a (ludicrously inappropriate) cliché.

Just as a beautiful face has been said to launch a thousand ships, a delicious, high-quality ham can launch a multitude of convenient, great-tasting meals.

The "face that launched a thousand ships" cliché would be bad enough. But likening Helen of Troy to pork butt—*that* is transcendentally bad. We promise we didn't make this up. The sentence actually began a story (enticingly entitled "Take Ham to New Heights") in an honest-to-goodness magazine.

> "The secret of good writing is to say an old thing in a new way or to say a new thing in an old way."
>
> —Richard Harding Davis

On the other hand, you can play with clichés, make them work for you by tweaking them just enough, as in this clever headline:

Chocolate Gets Hot But Holds Its Temper

The writer is playing a linguistic trick here based on a play on the word *temper*, which is both a noun meaning angry disposition and a verb describing the process of melting and reforming chocolate. If you knew that—and a decent percentage of readers of the Dining section of "The New York Times," where this headline appeared, would you would delight in this stylistic tidbit.

Play with Figures of Speech

Consider this clever and appropriate simile in a story about home makeover shows on TV:

Since "Trading Spaces" had its premiere on TLC ... copycats and variations on the idea have been multiplying like wire hangers in a walk-in closet.

Or how about this metaphor in the middle of a quirky feature about a man who collects antique toasters and opened a toaster museum:

Ten years ago, Norcross' toaster obsession was unshaped dough on the breadboard of his life.

Here is a movie reviewer describing the main character (Jeff Bridges) in the movie "Crazy Heart:"

He smokes and drinks as if trying to settle a long ago bet between his liver and his lungs about which he would destroy first.

What grabs us when we read these sentences, what makes us smile, is the unique vision, the odd, surprising or wonderfully apt comparisons. Similes are verbal comparisons that use *like* or *as* to announce themselves. Original similes have power, impact, even humor. Run-of-the-mill comparisons or clichés contribute nothing: *as black as night, as cool as a cucumber, hair like spun gold.* These comparisons lack verve and originality. Where is the imaginative stretch in *as black as night?* Night *is* black. What's the interesting comparison here? There is none.

Whereas similes are explicit comparisons using *like* or *as, metaphors* express a more direct comparison. Instead of stating that item A is "like" item B (a simile), a metaphor states that item A *is* item B. In the example above, the toaster collector's obsession was not *like* unshaped dough, it *was* unshaped dough.

When you attribute human characteristics, feelings or behaviors to non-human or inanimate objects, you are using a device called *personification.* As you walk down the aisle of your grocery store, a package of double choco-late chunk cookies "beckons" you. Cookies, of course, don't beckon. You've attributed a human quality to a bakery item. You've personified the package of cookies. In the description of the Jeff Bridges character you just read, his liver and his lungs did not actually bet on their respective demises. This is human behavior attributed to internal organs. This is personification.

If you are thinking to yourself, "Figures of speech are fine for poets and novelists, but I'm a *journalist*," think again. As the examples in this section show, media writers can and do use literary devices as part of original, styl-ish writing. As information consumers become increasingly inundated with media messages, it becomes even more important to craft your message in original and memorable ways by using similes, metaphors, analogies and personification.

Play with Words

When we first saw Bella and her pretty, dead guy, Edward, in "Twilight," the series hadn't been saga-fied yet.

Saga-fied isn't a word, of course. It's the result of a writer having fun with a word. Here's the tagline for an AT&T ad that takes on Verizon. The word play is simple and effective.

When you compare, there's no comparison.

Note the bit of linguistic fun the writer has in the next sentence:

For millions of vegetarians, *beef* is a four-letter word.

Here the word play turns on the accepted meaning of *four-letter word* as a curse word.

There's nothing fancy about what these writers have done. You will note no pyrotechnics. Word play need not be complicated or devastatingly witty to be effective. It need only be original, memorable and, of course, appropriate to the tone of the message.

Rhythm and Sound

Words march to a beat. Long sentences move gently, liltingly, picking up momentum as they flow. Short sentences create a staccato beat. Repetition of words or phrases can add accent and meter. Sentence construction communicates. Words may have power, but words set in rhythmic sentences have clout. Let's examine six components of rhythmic sentence construction: repetition, parallelism, sentence length, fragments and run-ons and the sounds of words.

Use Repetition

Purposeful repetition of words or phrases can add rhythm and grace to sentences. But like all stylistic devices, it should be used sparingly. Too much repetition leads to boredom and clunkiness.

In the following magazine essay, note the repetition of *I don't mean*:

I love the rain. I don't mean I grudgingly appreciate its ecological necessity. I don't mean I've learned to tolerate it. I don't mean I wait it out, flipping through the calendar to see how many more pages until the sun might break through. I mean I love it.

Repetition performs three stylistic functions here: It quickens the pace of the story by establishing a rhythm that pulls the reader from sentence to sentence; it creates smooth transitions; it sets up a mystery (What *does* the author mean?) that presumably the reader will want to read more about.

In tapping out a meter, repetition creates emphasis. The word or phrase you repeat assumes prominence and becomes a focal point. Repetition can be a powerful, dramatic and compelling technique. Perhaps that's why it is so often used in passionate, memorable speeches like Martin Luther King's "I Have a Dream" incantation.

Create Power with Parallelism

Parallelism is actually a kind of repetition, the repetition of grammatical patterns used to convey parallel or similar ideas. Parallelism is thus simultaneously a component of agreement, coherence and style. Parallelism has the potential to create rhythm, emphasis and drama as it clearly presents ideas or action. Consider the pleasant parallelism in both of these sentences, part of the opening paragraph of a column on food:

> **[Americans] optimistically purchase Emeril's cookware, download Daniel's recipes and watch cooking shows. Yet they eat breakfast in their cars, lunch at their desks and chicken from a bucket.**

Parallelism in the first sentence results from the verb/object construction (purchase cookware, download recipes, watch shows). The parallelism in the second sentence is a little more sophisticated because the writer, having established a pattern (breakfast, lunch) stays with the parallel structure but surprises you with the content.

Here's the opening sentence of a magazine profile. Note the insistent repetition of "and only," and how it creates rhythm and expectation as it pulls the reader through:

> **There are 3.5 million truckers in America, and only 200,000 of them are women, and only a fraction of them are black women, and only one of them is Sputter.**

Vary Sentence Length

Short sentences are naturally punchy, emphatic and dramatic; long sentences are naturally lilting, rolling and restful. Sentence length communicates just as surely as do the words within the sentence. Consider this excerpt from a blog about mothers and their teen daughters (www.myteenagewerewolf .com). Note the increasingly clipped sentences and their power to deliver a punch.

> **The WORST thing about being the mother of a teenage daughter is the daily drama. It gives you whiplash, a migraine. The emotional turbulence shakes you to the core. The stormy waters make you seasick. Her mercury rises and falls. You sweat and freeze. You question her sanity. You question your sanity. You curse.**

On the other hand, consider this single, lengthy, almost breathless sentence:

Following Pollock's death she had succumbed to opioid addiction, lost a suit against Pollock's estate to recover kitchen utensils and stereo equipment she claimed were her rightful property as his common-law wife, and finally, while driving her Saturn under the influence of methadone and Xanax, decapitated a pedestrian.

Note how sentence construction and sentence length almost lull the reader, making the surprise at the end even more surprising.

Take care with sentence length. If you construct a series of sentences of similar lengths, you run the risk of creating a plodding, deadening rhythm. If the sentences are all short, your prose may sound truncated and choppy, like a page from a children's book: "See the ball. The ball is green. Throw the ball." If the sentences are all long, the audience's attention may wander. Varying sentence length helps maintain interest while giving you the opportunity to use rhythm for drama and emphasis.

Here's another example of using sentence length to communicate. Note the relatively long sentences followed unexpectedly by a short clipped sentence at the end.

Duane Coop is standing 20 feet away from his practice target—a three-foot-diameter log with a painted red bull's-eye—throwing a two-and-a-half- pound, 32-inch double-bladed ax. The ax makes long, slow, end-over-end revolutions as it sails toward the target. Sprawled under the target, the family cat suns himself, listening without interest to the crack the six-inch blade makes as it slices into the log. The cat figures Duane won't miss. The cat's right.

Consider Fragments and Run-Ons

A fragment (an unfinished piece of a sentence) and a run-on (two or more complete sentences spliced together incorrectly) are grammatical errors. But certain grammatical rules can be bent by knowledgeable writers who are striving to achieve special effects. The rules against fragments and run-ons can occasionally be broken when you have a specific purpose in mind, when your audience (and editor) will stand for it and when the material warrants it. Of course, some forms, like blogs, lend themselves to a more conversational style that naturally includes fragments and run-ons. Advertising copywriters seem to be particularly fragment-happy. They can overdo it, creating choppy, confusing messages. On the other hand, they can use fragments effectively, as in this Toyota ad:

All science. No fiction.

Fragments can create excitement, set a quick pace and grab attention. Like short sentences—but even more so—they have a brisk, staccato beat. They can be dramatic and emphatic.

What does grammar have to do with text messaging?

Nothing.

And therefore, everything.

Unlike the staccato beat of fragments, run-ons can communicate a breathless, singsong rhythm. Depending on the words and ideas, a run-on can quicken the pace with a giddy rush of words or slacken the pace with a languid, rolling motion. Consider this run-on sentence from a "Washington Post" story about a Marine drill sergeant:

> **He is seething, he is rabid, he is wound up as tight as a golf ball with more adrenalin surging through his hypothalamus than a cornered slum rat, he is everything that these Marine recruits with their heads shaved to dirty nubs have ever feared or even hoped a drill instructor might be.**

That sentence rushes forth, as full of adrenalin as the drill sergeant.

Do remember that breaking grammatical rules is serious business and that there's an important distinction between breaking a rule purposefully and breaking a rule because you don't know the rule. Before you use fragments or run-ons, ask yourself these questions:

- Is the device appropriate to both the subject I am writing about and the medium I am writing for?

- Is this device the best way to achieve the effect for which I am striving?

- Does it work?

Don't use fragments or run-ons unless you can answer yes to all three questions. Even then use these techniques sparingly. Like all stylistic devices, they lose both meaning and impact when overused.

Listen to the Sounds of Words

"A sentence is not interesting merely in conveying a meaning of words; it must do something more," wrote poet Robert Frost, who ought to know. "It must convey a meaning by sound." Broadcast journalists, podcasters and speechwriters learn to write for the ear, but online and print writers often pay little attention to the sounds of the words they choose. That's unfortunate because most readers *hear* the word in their minds as they read. Print and online writers should be writing for the "inner ear" of their readers. Words chosen and arranged for their sound, as well as their meaning, add style and verve to prose.

Our language is full of words that sound like what they mean. Onomatopoeic words like *crack, buzz, snap, bang* and *chirp* imitate the sounds they define. They are crisp, colorful and doubly descriptive. Note how the "liveliness quotient" increases when you choose a word for its sound:

Instead of	Use
run	dash, dart, bolt, sprint
complain	grumble, squawk, growl
fracture	smash, shatter, snap
talk (a lot)	jabber, yammer, chatter

Some words are not actually onomatopoeic, but their sounds add to their meaning. Words beginning with the "s" sound, for example, often communicate (by sound and meaning) a kind of unpleasantness: *sneer, smirk* and *snigger* are stronger, nastier words than *mock, deride* or *look askance*. *Entanglements* can be *complications, problems* or *puzzles*, or they can be *snarls* or *snags*. A dog can *dribble* or *drool*, or it can (even more unpleasantly) *slobber* or *slaver*. The meanings are the same; sound adds the extra dimension.

In Chapter 8, we stressed the importance of choosing precise, accurate words. Here we are saying the writer striving for style ought to go one step further. Sound communicates. Look at both the meanings of words and their sounds.

Imagery

As writers, we are the eyes and ears of our audience. If we do our job well, we should be able to accurately re-create an event, a scene, a person, a moment in time for our audience. If we try harder, if we write with style, we can re-create in such vivid detail that our audience feels it has experienced what we write about. Including descriptive detail, showing rather than telling, and using quotations and anecdotes are all stylistic techniques that can bring the subject close to the audience.

Use Descriptive Detail

Remember the buildings at Tupperware headquarters that looked like plastic containers? This is descriptive detail. Descriptive detail does not mean a truckload of adjectives. It means a word, a phrase, a sentence or the makings of an entire scene that focuses on illuminating particulars.

Consider this description of a woman of another era:

She had style: the silk kerchief tied at the throat; the high heels she wore even to go grocery shopping; the straight skirts with kick pleats; the single eyebrow raised, a trick she perfected as a teenager after long hours in front of the mirror. She had beautiful eyebrows, high and arched, never plucked too thin. She had beautiful eyes, too, a clear, pale blue, with dark lashes that needed no mascara.

The details, carefully observed, bring the reader closer.

Descriptive detail can capture an action, help re-create an event or paint a scene. The writing need not be fancy. Plain, crisp language is your best ally, as in this description of a house:

Pancho's new house was on the outskirts of town on a half-acre of scorched dirt stubbled with desert weed and brush, an old wooden barn in back, a big, misshapen tamarisk tree in front. It was a squat, ugly, flat-roofed building made of chunks of rock set in concrete troweled over chicken wire. The rock was the color of dried blood.

Show, Don't Tell

When you *tell* the audience something, you stand between the audience and the subject to offer judgments.

> "Don't tell me the moon is shining; show me the glint of light on broken glass."
>
> —Anton Chekhov

Consider this flat statement:

Leah was a busy girl.

This "descriptive" sentence fails to describe. It summarizes the writer's conclusions instead of presenting details, images and concrete examples that would help readers draw their own conclusions. It *tells* rather than *shows*. Contrast it with this:

Leah rushed from basketball practice to a clarinet lesson, then to her a capella singing group, after which she studied her lines for the play, did two hours of French homework and cleaned her room.

Now *that's* busy. The details—not the writer's judgment—lead the reader to the conclusion.

Use Quotations

Lively, involving writing almost always includes people. One way to bring people to the forefront of a story is to let them talk, to quote them. A *quotation* is a verbatim statement—the words between the quotation marks are the actual words spoken by the person being quoted. During the information-gathering process, media writers may listen to speeches; attend meetings and conferences; interview by email, telephone or in person or stand in the background and listen to conversation. All the while they are scribbling notes or recording or both. When it comes to writing, they can be faced with pages and pages of quotations. How do they decide which to use and which to discard?

The first and most important consideration is *content*. Quoted material, like everything else the writer decides to include, should add to the audience's understanding of the message. The next consideration is *style*. Well-chosen quotations can be powerful elements in a story. They can:

- Bring the audience in direct contact with the person.

- Capture and communicate a person's uniqueness.

- Contribute to showing rather than telling.

- Bring personality and passion to issues (even "dull" ones).

- Make a person—and a story—come alive.

A well-chosen quotation clearly and vividly communicates something about the person. It is brief enough to hold the audience's interest. It expresses an idea that you, the writer, could not have said better. The last criterion is important. Sometimes people are long-winded; sometimes they go off on tangents. If you quote them (unless you are trying to show their long-windedness), you risk boring or confusing your audience. If the material is important enough to include, paraphrase it in your own words. Save quotations for strong, lively material.

But it's not just a quotation that can capture a person's uniqueness and enliven a story, it is how what was said was said—the context. The audience must be placed next to the person, must see and hear the person as he or she speaks. Consider the way quotations in context make this locker-room scene come alive:

The heat and the anger redden Jody's face as she stalks off the court and down to the locker room. She doesn't wait for the team to find seats on the long wooden bench before she starts in on them.

"You're making them look like goddamn all-Americans out there!" she screams. "You're dragging up and down the court with your tongues hanging out." She makes her voice whiny without lowering the decibel level. "*It's too hot and you're too tired*. I am just not interested in hearing that, ladies. You should never have let them back into the game. Never. Now go back out there and *play*."

Here's another example. Note how the writer incorporates the contextual material as she goes along. Description and quotation work hand in hand as the writer introduces the subject of this newspaper profile, then 90-year-old Alice Roosevelt Longworth:

"I still," she muses, rapping her bony fingers against her graying head, "more or less have my, what they call, marbles," and she pulls her flowered shawl around her a little closer, throws her head back and laughs gleefully.

This quotation does everything a good quotation should. The reader can *hear* the subject talking.

Use Anecdotes

An anecdote is a short account of an incident, a "mini story" with a beginning, middle and end. An anecdote illustrates a key point in the story, captures the essence of a character or highlights an important theme, offering detail and insight not possible any other way. It *shows* something the writer could have *told* but in the telling would have weakened. Anecdotes can require a major expenditure of words, and media writers are often strapped for space or time. That's why it is vital to choose wisely, selecting that one moment that reveals, unmasks or captures some important truth about the subject. Consider this anecdote from the book, "Dancing with Rose: Finding Life in the Land of Alzheimer's."

It's lunch break, but Lena is not eating. "You ought to eat something," I tell her.

"I got something out of the machine," she says. That means, at best, a bag of Doritos. I ask how, if she doesn't eat lunch, she keeps up her strength for working. She's forty-five but looks a hard sixty.

She shrugs. She smokes and watches me eat the salad I brought from home.

"I bought fresh vegetables once," she says. I nod encouragingly. She takes another drag. "Yeah, they stayed in the refrigerator until they rotted."

This anecdote illuminates Lena's character as it touches on the unhappy truth that caregivers often don't take care of themselves. Could the writer have just written that? Sure. But the telling is flat and colorless; the showing brings it to life. Well-told anecdotes are the product of superior observation and interviewing skills as well as sophisticated writing skills. They are tough to do but very much worth the effort. Like descriptive detail, quotations and other "show, don't tell" techniques, anecdotes add zest to your writing.

Writing with Style

"Rich, ornate prose is hard to digest, generally unwholesome and sometimes nauseating," writes E.B. White in the classic "Elements of Style." Lively, original, writing, on the other hand, is a delicately seasoned dish one can savor.

> "The hardest thing about writing, in a sense, is not writing. I mean, the sentence is not intended to show you off, you know. It is not supposed to be, 'Look at me!' 'Look, no hands!' It's supposed to be a pipeline between the reader and you."
>
> —James Baldwin

Writers spend their lives learning how to create irresistible prose. They read voraciously. They play with different ideas. They sweat the details. They make mistakes. They try again. They make more mistakes. But if they love their craft, and they love the language—and they have the patience and perseverance it takes—they (*you!*) can learn to write compelling, memorable prose.

For additional resources go to **www.cengagebrain.com**

PART 2

Your Speedy Grammar and Word Use Guide

Need the answer *now*? This is the place for concise answers to common grammatical and word use questions. However, these brief, alphabetical listings don't substitute for the fuller discussion you have in Part One.

Some style guides are unnecessarily authoritarian—"my way or the highway," if you will. Others are so permissive that they make anarchy seem like consensus-driven government. Here, we offer you guidance rather than firm prescriptions, respectful of tradition but aware of our language's dynamic nature.

Let's begin.

a/an These two articles often accompany nouns, but when do we use *a* rather than *an*? Your rule from grade school still stands, in our view: *a* precedes *almost all* nouns that begin with a consonant, as in "*a* book," but *an* is used with *all* nouns that begin with a vowel, as in "*an* oxymoron." Any exceptions? Well, the consonant *h* comes to mind. If you listen carefully, *h* has a relatively silent character, giving more authority to the vowel that follows it. So, we choose *an* for such *h* sounds as "*an* hour." What about "hat"? The *h* is more pronounced, hence, "*a* hat." Lest this all seem too cut and dried, consider the adjective "historic." The a/an choice there once pitted two famous journalists against each other on the op-ed section of "The New York Times." One chose "*a* historic moment," whereas the other defended "*an* historic moment." Our choice? Given the softness of that *h*, we pick *an*.

acronym It's a word (well, sort of) created by using the beginning letter or letters of a group of words, such as PAC (**P**olitical **A**ction **C**ommittee) and SONAR (**SO**und **NA**vigation and **R**anging). Creation of acronyms reflect the dynamism and inventiveness of our language. So, we have *scuba* (self-contained underwater breathing apparatus) as well as a term that recalls the days of luxurious transatlantic ships, *posh* (port outbound, starboard home). Who could forget the old military use of *snafu* (situation normal: ... well, you know).

Acronyms do not use periods between letters, unlike abbreviations that cannot be pronounced as a single word, such as A.C.L.U., the American Civil Liberties Union.

active voice/passive voice Voice refers to the form of a verb. When the subject of the sentence performs the action of the verb ("She wrote the story"), the verb *wrote* is in the active voice. If the subject receives the action ("The story was written by her"), the verb *was written* is in the passive voice. The active voice is always stronger and more direct than the passive voice. However, you might use passive voice when you need to stress the receiver of the action rather than the performer or when the performer is unknown (see p. 36.)

adapt/adopt *Adapt* refers to a "change to fit a situation" both in physical and conceptual ways:

> He **adapted** Norman's novel to a prime-time television series.

> The anthropologist quickly **adapted** to the customs of the tribe.

Adopt, however, denotes the action of "taking on," as in

> **Do you know why she adopted this "devil-may-care" attitude?**
> ("took on")

It also denotes "taking in," as in

> **The family adopted a black Labrador.**
> ("took in")

adverse/averse Although they sound alike, these adjectives have distinct meanings. *Adverse* means "unfavorable or hostile":

> **Investment bankers were surprised by the sudden onset of adverse economic conditions.**

If you want to describe someone's reluctance or opposition, you should use *averse*:

> **I am not averse to to the occasional but creative sentence fragment.**

advice/advise *Advice* is a noun denoting an "opinion," whereas *advise* is a verb that means "to counsel" or "to recommend." So, consider this sentence:

> **I advise you to ignore your astrologist's advice.**

affect/effect A pox on this pair! These words sound alike, but they are most often different parts of speech. *Affect* is *almost always* a verb that means "to have an impact on or "to influence" and in some cases "to pretend to have." *Effect* is *almost always* a noun that means "result" or "impact." For example:

> **This bill will adversely affect millions of welfare recipients.**
> (verb: "to have an impact on")

> **The defendant affected a carefree manner.**
> (verb: "to pretend to have")

> **Voters are questioning the effect of term limits.**
> (noun: "impact")

But just to make things interesting, *effect* is occasionally used as a verb in formal writing to mean "to bring about," and *affect* can be a noun in very narrow usage to denote certain behavior in psychology:

Top management _effected_ some personnel changes.
(verb: "brought about")

Michael's flat _affect_ concerned his psychologist.
(noun: "psychological state")

aid/aide Don't be fooled: Aides ("assistants") give aid ("help, assistance") to their bosses. _Aid_ also can be a verb, but _aide_ can only be a noun. So, constructions such as "the president's aide" and "giving aid and comfort to the enemy" are correct.

all ready/already By the end of this section, you should be all ready to avoid confusion between the adjective phrase _all ready_ and the adverb _already_. You are "completely prepared" to do something when _all_ modifies _ready_. But you've learned something "by now" or "by this time" when you know the meaning of the adverb _already_.
So:

Tom was _all ready_ to board the flight when his pager beeped.

Tom was _already_ on the plane when his pager beeped.

allude/elude These meanings shouldn't elude you. If you are making an _indirect_ reference to something, you allude to it. If you want to mention it directly, you refer to it.

The candidate _alluded_ to his opponent's lengthy prison record.

Elude is your choice if you mean "to escape or to avoid detection."

The fugitive _eluded_ the search party for two weeks.

a lot Yes, the word _lot_ can mean "a parcel of land." But the usual confusion with this casual phrase meaning "many" or "much" is its appearance as one word. It is not correct to write _alot_. Always use the phrase as two words.

I have seen _a lot_ of bad grammar errors in my time.

altar/alter The noun _altar_ is defined as "a table-like structure used in religious ceremonies." The verb _alter_ means "to change or modify." So:

The congregation voted to _alter_ the shape of the church _altar_.

among/between You may have learned this old rule: _among_ generally relates to more than two persons or things, and _between_ applies to only two. But it's not that simple. A more accurate guide is this: If there is a definite relation involved, _between_ is preferred, no matter what the number:

Between you and me, this movie will flop.

Negotiations have broken down <u>between</u> the government mediator, autoworkers and management.

Among is properly used when there is no explicit relationship stated and when distribution is stressed:

The reward was divided <u>among</u> five families.

antecedents Often hiding in a sentence like a snake in tall grass, an antecedent is the noun to which a pronoun refers. A clear connection between the antecedent and the pronoun is necessary for the sentence to make sense and read well. But sometimes the antecedent of a pronoun is unclear, causing problems with agreement between the antecedent and the verb. In the following sentences, proper antecedents are underlined:

Joe is one of those <u>people</u> who never take "no" for an answer.

Why is the antecedent *people* instead of *one*? Because the sentence indicates that more than one person will not take no for answer, the dependent clause needs the *plural* verb *take*.

<u>Jericho</u> is the only one of the finalists who isn't nervous.

In this sentence, only one finalist isn't nervous, hence the singular verb.

Sam's <u>theory</u> is intriguing, but not many of his colleagues agree with it.

The pronoun *it* properly refers to the antecedent *theory*. The intriguing theory, not Sam, is the focus.

a number of/the number of The intended number of these phrases depends on the article. If the article is *a*, the meaning is plural:

<u>A number</u> of budget issues <u>are</u> on today's agenda.

If the article is *the*, the meaning is more indefinite (or is seen as a unit) and therefore is singular:

<u>The number</u> of unemployment applications <u>is</u> increasing.

Here is an easy-to-remember tip about subject–verb agreement: If the phrase or word denotes a general amount or quantity, the verb is singular; if the phrase or word denotes a more definable number of individuals, the verb is plural (see pages 65 and 67).

anxious/eager Why are so many people *eager* to use *anxious* improperly? Are they anxious *about* writing too slowly? *Anxious* implies fear and worry:

County commissioners are <u>anxious</u> about this election.

If you are positively excited at the prospect of doing something, you are *eager* to do it:

Tom's fans are <u>eager</u> to meet him after the concert.

Note: You can be anxious *about* something; you *cannot* be anxious *to do* that thing!

anybody/anyone and any body/any one As compound words, *anybody* and *anyone* are indefinite pronouns that refer to no one in particular. As two separate words, they become adjective–noun combinations that are more pointed—one (person or thing) of a defined group.

<u>Anybody</u> can learn to swim with an attentive instructor.
(possible for all who are interested)

<u>Any one</u> of these players can be substituted in today's game.
(any player on the team)

It's common for *any one* to be followed by *of*. If you can insert a noun after an implied *of*, then the adjective–noun combination is a must.

appositive This is a word, phrase or clause that restates or adds information about the word that precedes it. Words in apposition have a side-by-side relationship. They are important to identify because they have some bearing on punctuation and case decisions. For example, a restrictive appositive is one that is essential to the meaning of a sentence and thus requires no commas:

My friend <u>John</u> helped write copy while his friend <u>Jerril</u>
          (appos.)   (appos.)

did the design.

(A comma would not be correct after *friend* because John and Jerill are essential to the meaning of the subject.)

A nonrestrictive appositive still has a side-by-side relationship, but its meaning is not essential to the sentence. It must be set off by commas:

Robinson, <u>a proven clutch player</u>, won a secure place on the roster.
          (appos.)

as if/like These are not interchangeable. *As if* acts as a conjunction and introduces a clause:

It looks <u>as if</u> it will rain.

Like, a preposition, takes a simple object and cannot introduce a clause:

It looks <u>like</u> rain.

Some grammarians say that *like* may evolve into a conjunction. (We're not holding our breath.)

as/than   Because *as* and *than* can be both prepositions and conjunctions, case selection may be tricky. If these words are used as conjunctions, they are most likely to make comparisons. If so, the nominative case of the pronoun is needed:

There's no one more handsome <u>than</u> he.

In the example above, *than he is handsome* is understood as the second clause.

However, *as* and *than* can also be prepositions:

Why did you pick Brutus rather <u>than</u> her?

Obviously, no comparison is being made here. The pronoun following the preposition must be in the objective case.

as well as   This phrase, which connects a subordinate thought to the main one, can cause agreement problems between subject and verb. Remember that the main subject—not any word or phrase parenthetical to it—controls the number and the person of the verb:

The house, <u>as well as</u> its two storage sheds, is scheduled for demolition.

Similar parenthetical phrases are *together with, in addition to* and *along with*. You'll find it easier to isolate the true subject of the sentence if you set off these phrases with commas (see p. 65).

aural/oral   You will see this pair in Appendix A on homonyms and homophones. We cite them as an example of the need to understand the distinctions between words that have similar pronunciations but very different meanings and spellings. As with other homonyms and homophones, if you only hear the word and never see it on a page or a screen, correct use (and spelling) can be a challenge. So—*aural* refers to *hearing*, whereas *oral* refers to *speaking*. Please note all entries in Appendix A and be alert to their significant differences in meaning.

bad/badly   Don't feel bad if you use these words badly! *Bad* is an adjective. In linking-verb constructions in which you want to describe the subject (either a noun or a pronoun), *bad* is the correct choice:

The mayor <u>feels</u> <u>bad</u> about recent council discord.
        (l.v.) (adj.)

This sentence describes the mayor's state of mind, not his physical ability to feel. When you describe some quality of the verb instead of the subject, you use the adverb *badly*:

> **The prime minister took her defeat <u>badly.</u>**

Here, *badly* describes the verb *took*, not the noun *prime minister*.)

because of/due to   Use *because of* when matching cause to effect. It is used when the writer can ask *why* in a sentence:

> **He was fired <u>because</u> he constantly missed deadlines.**

Due to should be used only in a linking verb construction. *Due* is an adjective; its preposition *to* relates to the condition of a subject:

> **The increase in the cost of burritos is <u>due to</u> rising prices of jack cheese.**

Note that you can't ask why in this construction, but you can in the next, which is why *because of*, not *due to*, is correct:

> **<u>Because of</u> the budget crunch this year, a number of part-time positions will be eliminated.**

beside/besides   *Beside* means "next to" or "at the side of." *Besides* means "in addition to":

> **Please stand <u>beside</u> your sister during the ceremony.**
> (next to)

> **<u>Besides</u> you and me, only Captain America knows the location of the**
> (in addition to)
> **hideout.**

Both *beside* and *besides* are prepositions, so remember that simple objects of prepositions always take the objective case.

bi-/semi-   *Bi-* means "two," and *semi-* means "half." Stick with these distinctions. *Bimonthly* means "every two months"; *semimonthly* means "twice a month." If you are referring to something that happens twice a year, use *semiannual* rather than *biannual*, even though the dictionary recognizes both. That will avoid confusion with *biennial* (something that happens every two years). Note that words containing the prefixes *bi-* and *semi-* are hyphenated only when the root word (the word the prefix attaches to) begins with an *i* or is capitalized.

both/few/many/several   These are indefinite pronouns, and when they are subjects of sentences, they always take a plural verb (see p. 67).

brand names/trademarks These are business-created words that have not fallen into generic usage. Do you really want to refer to a specific product, or do you just want to mention the process? If you want to mention the process or the generic name, avoid brand name reference. Do not write, for example:

The spy <u>xeroxed</u> all the documents.

For one thing Xerox, a registered trade name, isn't a verb; the spy can photocopy the documents, but he or she can't xerox, canonize or savinize them. Other examples are Scotch tape (a brand of cellophane tape), ChapStick (a lip balm), Mace (a brand of tear gas), Jell-o (a gelatin dessert) and Kleenex (a brand of facial tissue). All brand names and trademarks should be capitalized. Over the years, U.S. courts have declared a brand name to be generic, as with aspirin (now written in lower case). What do you think the courts will say about this phrase: "I'll *google* it."

bureaucratese/jargon Jargon has changed our language—but not for the better. These words and phrases, used by government workers, scientists, doctors, computer programmers and a host of other professionals, usually do more to obscure than to clarify. For example, you no longer measure the effect of deficit spending on a budget; you "ascertain how the program will impact fiscal planning." You no longer evaluate things; you "effect a needs assessment." A heart attack becomes an "M.I." (myocardial infarction). When these professionals talk to one another, their language may be both efficient and precise. But when journalists write for broader audiences, this specialized language does not work (see p. 109).

but *But* is most frequently a conjunction, connecting words and phrases of equal rank and implying a contrast between those elements. *But* almost always requires a comma between the clauses it separates:

That tune is catchy, <u>but</u> you can't dance to it.

But also can be a preposition meaning "except":

Everybody <u>but</u> me went to the party.

Note that the objective case is required for the pronoun.

Can *but* be used to begin a sentence, like the conjunctive adverb *however*? But of course—if you don't overdo it.

can/may *Can* denotes ability, and *may* denotes possibility and permission. If your sentence is in the form of a question, *may* is almost always your choice:

<u>May</u> I go to the exhibit?
(Permission, not ability, is the focus.)

Do you think I <u>can</u> win this election?
(Do I have the ability to win?)

Some stylebook authorities have thrown in the towel on the interchange-ability of *can* and *may*, but we're not willing to give up the fight. However, remember that *may* can also express a possibility.

I <u>may</u> buy that new boat we've been talking about.

case   *Who* or *whom? We* or *us?* Understanding case helps us make these grammatical choices. The three cases are nominative, objective and posses-sive. Certain pronouns change their form to accommodate a change in case. Nouns change only in their possessive case (see pp. 78–79).

capital/capitol   The distinction (related to government) is simple: The capi-tal is the city in which a state government is headquartered, as in Columbus, Ohio. The building where state government meets to legislate is called the capitol, although the term *statehouse* is also used. Of course, we have other meanings for capital, as in "money/assets," "uppercase letters" and, to cite the Brits, "great," as in "That's a *capital* idea!"

censor/censure   These words have different meanings, pronunciations and spellings, so what's the confusion? Perhaps it's because the meanings are inter-related. You can censor *materials* by screening, changing or forbidding them.

The general <u>censored</u> all dispatches from the battle lines.

You generally can censure only people—by condemning them or expressing disapproval of their actions.

The senators <u>censured</u> their colleague because he <u>censored</u> a staff report.

These words can also be nouns. So, you can have an "official government censor" as well as a "resolution of censure."

chair/chairperson   The term *chairman* incorrectly assumes maleness of that position. It is one of many such terms in our language (others are *policeman* and *businessman*). For years, authoritative dictionaries have defined *chair* as "a person who presides over a meeting" and "an office or position of authority." A person—man or woman—can chair a meeting or be a program chair. It as-sumes nothing but the position itself. *Chairperson* seems a bit more awkward to us, but it may be what an organization chooses to call its leader.

cite/site/sight   These homophones have nothing in common except their pronunciation. You make reference to a person or thing when you *cite*, to a piece of land when you are on *site*, or to a visual spectacle when you *sight*.

Cite is always a verb:

> **The proclamation <u>cited</u> the bravery of three teenagers during the Bronxville fire.**

Site is always a noun, though there is evidence that some writers probably influenced by architects, are trying to use it as a verb:

> **The <u>site</u> of the 1964 World's Fair used to be a garbage dump.**

But you can *sight* (verb) or have *sight* (noun):

> **She <u>sighted</u> the island from the ship after thinking that none was**
> (verb: saw)

> **in <u>sight.</u>**
> (noun: a view)

clause   This is a group of words that contains both a subject and a verb. An independent clause expresses a complete thought and can stand alone. A dependent clause has a subject and a verb, but the meaning is incomplete, and therefore cannot stand alone as a sentence (see p. 23).

collective nouns   They look singular (*jury, herd, committee*) but imply plurality. Or they can look plural (*athletics, politics*) but imply singularity. What's a writer to do? Here's the answer: If the noun is considered as a whole, the verb and associated pronouns are singular:

> **The jury <u>was</u> seated this morning.**

> **Politics <u>is</u> a dirty business.**

If the unit is broken up or considered individually, the plural verb is required (see p. 68):

> **The herd of cattle <u>have</u> scattered.**

> **The senator's politics <u>are</u> changeable.**

collision   This is a violent contact between moving bodies. An accident between a moving car and a stationary telephone pole is not a collision; it is a crash. But an oil tanker might collide with a frigate on the high seas. In a more figurative sense, ideas, opinions and, yes, words can collide (perhaps more significantly than violently)!

colon   This punctuation mark (:) introduces thoughts, quotations, examples or a series. Capitalize matter following a colon only if it can stand alone as a sentence:

Her parting words inspired them for years: "You must think outside the box."

Besides cartooning, Charles Schulz had one great passion: hockey.

comma splice Also known as a *comma fault*, this occurs when the writer improperly joins two independent clauses without either a coordinating conjunction or a semicolon:

A 10-vehicle pileup blocked the interstate highway, state officials estimate it won't reopen for two days.

The example above lacks the conjunction *but* or a semicolon between clauses and creates what is also known as a run-on sentence.

He enjoys reviewing movies, however, he says he can't waste his time on "trash like this."

In this sentence, the presence of the conjunctive adverb *however* requires a semicolon between clauses—that is, between *movies* and *however*.

In short sentences, the comma splice receives the blessing of most grammarians. "You'll like him, he's a Taurus" can survive without a conjunction or a semicolon. An accomplished writer who does not want the harsh stop of a semicolon to slow the meter of a sentence might employ the comma splice as a stylistic tool.

comparative/superlative refers to the "degrees" of certain adjectives and adverbs. Let's take the word *smart* and examine its degrees as an adjective (*smart*) and adverb (*smartly*):

smart (adj.)	smarter *(comparative)*	smartest *(superlative)*
smartly (adv.)	more smartly *(comparative)*	most smartly *(superlative)*

Obviously, when you establish a comparative degree for an adjective, it is redundant to attach an adverb to it as well, as in *more smarter*.

compared to/compared with Their meanings are about as interchangeable as feet and meters. When you liken one thing to another, you *compare* it *to*:

The mayor's behavior can be compared to that of a 3-year-old in the throes of a tantrum.

When you place items side by side to examine their similarities and differences, use *compared with*:

Compared with housing prices 10 years ago, real estate costs today seem like a bargain.

The use of *compared to* is both figurative and metaphorical. *Compared with*, on the other hand, is statistical rather than creative.

complement/compliment Both can be nouns or verbs. *Complement* means "that which completes something, supplements it or brings it to perfection." *Compliment* means "an expression of praise or admiration." So, a necklace might complement a blouse, but you would compliment the wearer on her good taste in necklaces.

compose/comprise *Compose* is not as direct as *comprise*. Something is *composed of* other things ("made up of"); however, one thing *comprises* ("takes in, includes") other things. The following are correct usages:

> **Her recipe for success is <u>composed of</u> hard work, creative thought and manageable risk.**

> **His speech <u>comprises</u> three familiar themes.**

As you can see from the last example, the *whole* (speech) comprises (includes) the *parts* (themes). A whole is never comprised of the parts. That would be the same as saying (nonsensically) that "the whole is included of its parts."

compound modifiers These are two adjectives or an adverb joined to an adjective to modify a noun. Often a hyphen is needed to join these modifiers to make the meaning clear:

> <u>well-reasoned</u> <u>argument</u>

> <u>hard-driving</u> perfectionist

Modifiers do not require a hyphen if they are preceded by *very* or an *-ly* adverb. These adverbs obviously modify what follows, and there is no mistaking their connection:

> <u>very dedicated</u> teacher

> <u>highly motivated</u> worker

Don't string together too many modifiers in the name of description and economy. All you'll get is clutter. If you find yourself having to tack on two or more modifiers, you probably have chosen the wrong word. Try searching for the one word, if possible, that means just what you want to say (see p. 129).

conjunction The conjunction links words, phrases and clauses; if used properly, it provides both logic and rhythm to a sentence. Note how the conjunction *and* provides parallelism or equality to a clause:

The border guard quickly stamped the passport <u>and</u> cheerfully directed the tourist to the nearest town.

But (what a great conjunction—it provides a contrast or shows a lack of unity) note how the conjunction *and* is used improperly when it links obviously unrelated elements in a sentence:

She refuses to work overtime, <u>and</u> she is a great crossword puzzle solver.

The pairing of these two clauses is unfortunate *and* hurts the flow.

conjunctive adverb Words like *however, therefore* and *nevertheless* may look like conjunctions, but they are really adverbs. Why is this distinction important? It's because conjunctive adverbs need a semicolon—not a comma (as conjunctions do)—to link sentence parts (see pp. 91–92). For example:

Your writing needs more clarity; <u>however</u>, I think your main argument is persuasive.

continual/continuous *Continual* means "repeated or intermittent." *Continuous* means "unbroken":

Must I suffer these <u>continual</u> interruptions?

The parched hiker imagined a <u>continuous</u> line of canteens stretched across the barren horizon.

contraction It's a generally successful and sensible merging of words for economy and informality. Examples: *It's* (it is), *who's* (who is), *doesn't* (does not). We use the apostrophe to span the missing letter or letters. **Don't overdo it—it'd (it would) quickly get out of hand!**

convince/persuade If you think these words are identical in meaning, we're just going to have to *persuade* you that they're not. We'll do that until you're *convinced*! To begin with, people do not convince others of anything; that action is persuasion:

Can you <u>persuade</u> Helen to change her vote?

To be convinced is to be secure in a decision or a principle.

I'm <u>convinced</u> that Helen won't change her mind.

If a person attempts to persuade another and is successful, the first person is considered persuasive. Obviously the argument has been convincing. The process is to persuade; the hoped-for result is to be convinced. Got that now? Convinced? Or do you need to be persuaded?

council/counsel The difference between *counsel* (a verb or noun, depending on use in a sentence) and *council* (always a noun) is "one to many." When you seek *counsel*, you generally pursue advice from one person, such as an attorney or schoolteacher. But when you look to a *council*, you attend the meetings or hear the deliberations of a body of elected or appointed officials. Three examples:

The teacher <u>counseled</u> her students to carefully review the
    (verb)

sample exam.

I have always appreciated his thoughtful <u>counsel</u>.
                                     (noun)

The city <u>council</u> will meet tonight.
    (noun)

damage/destroy *Destruction* is the severest form of *damage*. Therefore, it is redundant to write "the building was completely destroyed in the fire." Anything less than destruction is simply a category of damage, as in

The fire caused only minor <u>damage</u> to the mayor's office.
(Note that *damage* can be a noun as well as a verb. That is not the case with *destroy—destruction* is its noun.)

Destruction needs no intensification:

The hurricane <u>destroyed</u> 40 homes and severely <u>damaged</u> 100 others.

dangling modifiers A modifier "dangles" when it does not directly modify anything in the sentence. For example:

Facing indictment for insider trading, the board demanded Stewart's resignation.

The participial phrase *facing indictment for insider trading* has nothing to modify. The first referent we see is *the board*, which is not facing indictment. Poor sentence construction has buried the true referent—the person who is facing indictment. The sentence needs to be rewritten:

<u>Facing indictment</u> for insider trading, <u>Stewart</u> announced his resignation this morning.

Dangling modifiers most often occur at the beginnings of sentences. Although they tend to be verbals (participial phrases, gerund phrases and infinitive phrases), appositives, clauses and simple adjectives can dangle as well. The test is whether the person or thing being modified by the word, phrase or clause is in the sentence (see p. 56).

dash An enticing piece of punctuation because of its informality, directness and drama, the dash (—) is often used excessively and incorrectly. Media writers should consider routinely using commas, colons and parentheses, and save dashes for special occasions. The two main uses of the dash in media writing are as follows:

1. To create drama and emphasis at the end of a sentence:

    The film was beautifully photographed and expertly directed—but it was a box office flop.

2. To clearly set off a long clause or phrase that adds information to the main clause:

    The closing ceremonies of the Olympics—a dazzling spectacle of international patriotism—sent the network's ratings through the roof.

data and other foreign plurals Many English words have their roots in Latin; some are derived from Greek. Some of these words conform to singular–plural rules unlike our own. *Data, media* and *alumni* are common Latin plurals. Magazines are one *medium*; *Facebook* and *Twitter are social media*. The word *alumni* presents its own complications: A group of men and women who have graduated from a school are *alumni*; one male graduate is an *alumnus*; one female grad is an *alumna*. And to be perfectly correct, a group of female grads would be *alumnae*. The Greek words *criteria* and *phenomena* are plural. Their singulars are *criterion* and *phenomenon*.

Data can be a confusing word. It's plural but when it can be considered as a cohesive unit, as a collective noun, it should take a singular verb:

Your data on yesterday's exit polling <u>is</u> impressive.
(unit)

If the sense of *data* is individual items, however, use a plural verb:

The data <u>were collected</u> from seven tracking sites.
(individual items)

dependent clause Although it contains both a subject and verb, a dependent clause does not express a complete thought and cannot stand alone as a sentence. Dependent clauses rely on main clauses for their completion:

Because the tax levy failed
(dep. clause)

Because the tax levy failed, <u>most city parks will be closed this summer</u>.
(dep. clause linked to underlined indep. clause)

Recognizing dependent clauses will help you (1) avoid fragments (treating dependent clauses as if they were complete sentences) and (2) vary sentence structure. To vary sentence structure, place the dependent clause in front, in the middle or at the end of the main clause (see p. 26).

desert/dessert You'd be surprised how often these words are confused, even though their pronunciations are so different. Desert can be noun or verb. As a noun, it refers to arid land, as in the *Sahara Desert*. As a verb, it means to abandon, run away or withdraw, as in

He <u>*deserted*</u> his guard post.

On the other hand, the noun *dessert* is far more pleasant—and even tasty, as in

Try any <u>**dessert**</u> with chocolate, and you'll be happy.

different from/different than Here's a promise: Use *different from* and you will never be wrong. Unless you're interested in delving into the nether regions of structural linguistics or semantic compatibility, consider using *different than* only when it introduces a condensed clause (a clause that omits certain words without loss of clarity).

Open-meeting laws are <u>**different**</u> in Illinois <u>**than**</u>
[they are] in Oregon.
(condensed clause)

In general, however, play it safe with *different from*. So the previous example would read:

Open-meeting laws in Oregon are different from those in Illinois.

differ from/differ with People who *differ from* ("are unlike") others may not necessarily *differ with* ("disagree with") each other. The terms are not interchangeable. When you mean two items are dissimilar, use *differ from*. When you mean items are in conflict, use *differ with*:

The competing proposals did not significantly <u>**differ from**</u> one another.

City councilors <u>**differed with**</u> the zoning committee's
recommendations.

discreet/discrete Both of these words are adjectives, and both are pronounced the same. But they do have discrete meanings! *Discreet* means "prudent or careful," especially about keeping confidences, as in this sentence:

The diplomat is known to be <u>**discreet**</u> in all matters.

DE-DI

Discrete means "distinct or separate," as in this sentence:

Desert and dessert have <u>discrete</u> meanings.

disinterested/uninterested If you are impartial about an issue, you would rightly be called *disinterested*. If you simply don't care or couldn't give the proverbial rip about it, then you are *uninterested*. Interesting distinction, yes?

drug A drug is any substance used as medicine in the treatment of a disease. Some writers have made the general term *drug* synonymous with narcotics, a particular group of sense-dulling, usually addictive drugs. All narcotics are drugs; however, all drugs are *not* narcotics.

either ... or/neither ... nor Called *correlative conjunctions*, these word pairs (including *both ... and, not so ... as*, and *not only ... but also*) connect similar grammatical elements in parallel form:

You can <u>either</u> pay the fine <u>or</u> go to jail.

These pairs can pose agreement problems. When a compound subject is linked by a correlative conjunction, the subject closest to the verb determines the number of the verb:

<u>Neither</u> the researcher <u>nor</u> her <u>assistants</u> <u>were</u> available for comment.

When the subject closest to the verb is singular, you must use a singular verb. Such a construction is grammatical but sometimes graceless:

<u>Neither</u> the assistants <u>nor</u> the <u>researcher</u> <u>was</u> available for comment.

Avoid awkwardness when possible by placing the plural subject next to the verb.

elicit/illicit *Elicit*, a verb, means "to bring out or draw forth." *Illicit*, an adjective, means "illegal or unlawful."

The mayor's <u>illicit</u> behavior <u>elicited</u> strong community reaction.

eminent/imminent These adjectives describe very different qualities. *Eminent* means "distinguished or prominent":

The <u>eminent</u> scientist Linus Pauling won two Nobel Prizes.

Imminent means "about to occur" or "impending":

The company faces <u>imminent</u> bankruptcy.

energize/enervate Here is an example of two words that may seem similar but that actually have opposed meanings. To *energize* is "to invigorate or give energy to." *Enervate*, on the other hand, means "to weaken or deplete." So:

Terri's optimism <u>energizes</u> everyone.

Simon's cynicism <u>enervates</u> even the most cheerful optimist.

enormity/enormousness These words are not synonymous, though recent usage (even by a U.S. president) would indicate otherwise. Although the pair starts with similar pronunciations, the differences are clear. *Enormity* means "wickedness." *Enormousness* refers to size.

The <u>enormity</u> of the 9-11 attacks is still difficult to comprehend.

The <u>enormousness</u> of the budget deficit has quieted even the most cynical politicians.

Perhaps some writers find *enormousness* a bit graceless and odd sounding. Fine. They should use *magnitude* rather than improperly suggesting horror or wickedness.

ensure/insure These verbs could be considered distant relatives in terms of meaning, but insure has a far more technical (and business) meaning than ensure. Here are two sentences that should illustrate their differences:

This study program will <u>ensure</u> your success in college.
("make certain, guarantee")

Please promise that you will <u>insure</u> that jalopy before you drive it.
("provide insurance coverage")

everyone/everybody These collective pronouns are troublesome because they "feel" plural even though they are actually singular.

<u>Everyone</u> should remain in his or her seat.

It is common to see and hear the incorrect plural: "Everyone should remain in *their* seats." Don't make that mistake! Also, in keeping this construction in the singular, remember fairness and accuracy. If all people included in *everyone* are male, then it is fine to write: "Everyone should remain in *his* seat." If the group is mixed, gender inclusivity needs to be reflected in the pronoun choice. If you think *his or her* is awkward, you can always rewrite, as in:

All <u>theater-goers</u> should remain in <u>their</u> seats.

farther/further Use *farther* to express physical distance (think "far"); use *further* when referring to degree, time or quantity:

> **The planning commission wants to extend the boundaries <u>farther</u> south.**

> **The planning commission will discuss the boundary issue <u>further.</u>**

Any questions? We'd be happy to discuss this further.

fewer/less This is a much-abused pair, but the distinctions are clear: When you refer to a number of individual items, *fewer* is your choice; when you refer to a bulk, amount, sum, period of time or concept, use *less*:

> **<u>Fewer</u> doctors result in <u>less</u> medical care.**

> **At Data Corporation <u>fewer</u> than 10 employees make <u>less</u> than $50,000 per year.**

In the latter example, we are not talking about individual dollars, but rather a unit of money.

One more example:

> **<u>Fewer</u> grammatical errors will result in <u>less</u> grief in this class.**

flaunt/flout Whether you flaunt or flout, you are overtly acting up with these verbs. When you "outrageously or pretentiously display," you *flaunt*. When you "scorn rules and laws," you *flout*.

> **She seems to enjoy <u>flaunting</u> her newfound wealth.**

> **The farmer <u>flouted</u> the law that prohibited raising turkeys within city limits.**

fragments An unfinished piece of a sentence, a fragment may be a single word, a phrase or a dependent clause. It may lack a subject, a predicate, a complete thought or any combination of the three. Therefore, a fragment is not a complete sentence; it cannot stand alone. Example:

> **Watching the moon rise in late summer.**
> (Where's the verb?)

Let's fix this:

> **He <u>enjoys</u> watching the moon rise in late summer.**
> (verb)

So why isn't "watching" a verb? (See p. 46.)

However, fragments are used purposefully by skillful writers. With their clipped, punchy beat, fragments can create excitement and grab readers' attention. But this stylistic device must be appropriate to both subject and medium, and should be used sparingly.

gender-specific references (he/she) Language reflects culture and beliefs. When a society changes, we believe language ought to keep pace. We speak not of faddish words or slang expressions, but of the way language treats people. The language in the following sentences is not an accurate reflection of our society:

A nurse ought to be attentive to <u>her</u> patients.

A governor has a responsibility to <u>his</u> constituents.

In these sentences we see outdated gender stereotypes—nurses are all female, elected officials are all male. Because the singular neuter pronoun (*it, its*) cannot refer to a person, we have two grammatical options if we want to avoid gender stereotyping:

1. Use both the masculine and the feminine pronoun when referencing a noun that could refer to either sex:

   A <u>nurse</u> ought to be attentive to <u>his or her</u> patients.

2. Change the neuter noun to the plural, and use plural neuter pronouns (*they, them, their*):

   Governors have a responsibility to <u>their</u> constituents.

In your effort to treat both sexes fairly in language, don't fall prey to easy (and incorrect) solutions that accept errors in agreement:

<u>Everybody</u> deserves to make it on <u>their</u> own.

This may be well-intentioned, but it is grammatically incorrect. Two solutions are obvious:

<u>Everybody</u> deserves to make it on <u>his or her</u> own.

<u>All people</u> deserve to make it on <u>their</u> own.

good/well If you understand the role of linking verbs and adverbs, you will know when to use the adjective *good* and the adverb *well*. A linking verb establishes a relationship between the subject and a modifier. When the subject of the sentence is linked to positive or desirable traits, then use the modifier *good*:

Future hiring prospects are <u>good.</u>

When the verb reflects an action properly, skillfully, or sufficiently, use the adverb *well*:

The old dog <u>performed</u> his new tricks <u>well.</u>
(performed how?)

So, stick to *good* for relating to subjects and *well* for characterizing verbs. Another example:

The doctors said she was <u>doing</u> <u>well</u> after the surgery.

(doing how?)

hanged/hung The verb *hang* is conjugated differently depending on the object of the hanging. The conjugation *hang, hung, hung* refers to objects:

The stolen Matisse <u>hung</u> in a dark corner of the hotel lobby for twenty years before being discovered.

The conjugation *hang, hanged, hanged* refers to people (executions or suicides):

The prisoner was <u>hanged</u> at midnight in the penitentiary basement.

hardy/hearty If you are strong and can endure challenges and hardships, consider yourself a *hardy* soul. Whether you are hardy or not, if you enjoyed some healthy and nutritious food, you will have had a *hearty* meal. If you have greeted someone with enthusiasm and even affection, you will have offered a *hearty* greeting. Nice adjectives, those.

historic/historical These adjectives both deal with history, but their difference is significant. When something is historic, it has particular importance to history, as in

The Rev. Martin Luther King's "I have a dream" address in 1963 is considered an <u>historic</u> speech.

Historical is a more general reference, connected to anything that is related to history, as in

Sarah enjoys reading <u>historical</u> novels.

homophones, homonyms and homographs If you're looking for more reasons to love the English language—or lose patience with it—look no further. Homophones are words that sound the same but are spelled differently and have unrelated meanings, like *fair* and *fare, alter* and *altar* and *whose* and *who's*. Homonyms are words that sound the same and are spelled the same, but—oddly—have completely different meanings, as in *stable* ("horse stall") and *stable* ("unwavering"). As if this were not enough, homographs are spelled the same but—maddeningly—are pronounced differently (and have different meanings), as in *bow* (in archery) and *bow* (of a ship). Please see Appendix A for quite a list of them!

hopefully Possibly the single most abused word in our language, *hopefully* means "with hope." It describes how a subject feels (hopeful). Therefore, this sentence is correct:

> She opened the mailbox <u>hopefully</u>, looking for her acceptance letter from Yale.

Hopefully—regardless of what you may hear or read—does not mean "it is hoped that." Therefore, the following sentence is incorrect:

> <u>Hopefully</u>, the check will arrive.

The check is not "hopeful." *Hopefully* does not describe anything in the preceding sentence. It is, in fact, a dangling modifier.

hyphen Whereas the dash creates a dramatic break in a sentence, the workhorse hyphen creates a typographical bridge that links words for several purposes.

1. It joins compound modifiers unless one of the modifiers is *very* or an *-ly* adverb:

   a <u>well-known</u> actor
   (hyphen needed)

   the <u>newly appointed</u> ambassador
   (*-ly* adverb, no hyphen needed)

2. It links certain prefixes to the words that follow. A guideline: If the prefix ends in a vowel and the next word begins with the same vowel, hyphenate (except *cooperate* and *coordinate*). It's best to check a dictionary or stylebook on this rule because exceptions abound (see p. 98). Some examples:

   the <u>pre-election</u> suspense

   but:

   a <u>precursor</u> of the election results

3. It links words when a preposition is omitted:

   score of <u>10–1</u>
   (preposition *to* omitted)

   closed <u>June–August</u>
   (preposition *through* omitted)

***-ics* words** Words ending with the suffix *-ics* (*athletics, politics, graphics, acoustics, economics*) can create problems with agreement. Although their final *s* makes these words look plural, they can be either singular or plural, depending on context. If the word refers to a science, art or general field of study, it is treated as singular and takes a singular verb. If the word refers to the act, practices or activities of the field, it takes a plural verb:

<u>Politics is</u> an impossible career.
(the field of politics, singular)

His <u>politics seem</u> to change every year.
(the practice of politics, plural)

Some *-ics* words do not carry both meanings. *Hysterics*, for example, always takes the plural because it always refers to acts and practices.

if I were   The *subjunctive mood* of verbs expresses a nonexistent or improbable condition. That mood calls for what may seem grammatically incorrect—a plural verb with a singular subject. But this sentence is grammatically correct:

<u>If I were</u> the world's richest person, all medical care would be free.

If you want to express a condition that is possible, however, it would be correct to say:

<u>If I was</u> plant supervisor, our productivity would increase.

if/whether   These conjunctions are not interchangeable. *If* means "in the event that," "granting that" or "on the condition that." It is often used to introduce a possibility or a hypothetical situation:

<u>If</u> Oakland wins today, the Raiders get home field advantage in
(a possibility)
the playoffs.

<u>If</u> the volcano were to erupt again, thousands of lives could be lost.
(hypothetical condition—note that the plural verb creates the subjunctive mood)

Whether means "if it is so that," "if it happens that," or "in case." It is generally used to introduce a possibility:

He wondered <u>whether</u> he should attend the briefing.
(if it is so that)

<u>Whether</u> she wins or loses, this will be her last political campaign.
(introduces possibilities)

impact   This noun means a "collision" or a "violent or forceful striking together." Often writers use *impact* when they really mean something much less forceful, such as "effect" or "influence."

The <u>impact</u> of the collision threw her from the vehicle.
(correct)

We can't predict what <u>impact</u> this report will have on future
(misuse—better to use *effect* or *influence*)
negotiations.

Unfortunately, *impact* has also fallen prey to those who toss it around as a verb ("The televised debates <u>impacted</u> the election") or an adjective ("federally <u>impacted</u> areas"). The only thing that can be impacted is a tooth, and that's unpleasant enough!

imply/infer   These verbs are not interchangeable. *Imply* means "to suggest or hint." *Infer* means "to deduce or conclude from facts or evidence."

When she <u>implied</u> that Smith was unethical, her supervisor <u>inferred</u> that she had an ax to grind.

indefinite pronouns   Because indefinite pronouns (*anyone, everyone, few, some* and so on) don't always specify a number, they can cause agreement problems. Here are a few rules to follow.

- When used as subjects, *each, either, anyone, everyone, much, no one, nothing* and *someone* always take a singular verb.

- Acting as subjects, *both, few, many* and *several* always take a plural verb.

- Pronouns such as *any, none* and *some* take singular verbs when they refer to a unit or general quantity. If they refer to amount or individuals, they take a plural verb (see p. 69):

<u>Some</u> of the shipment <u>was</u> delayed
(general quantity)

because <u>some</u> of the workers <u>were</u> on strike.
(individuals)

independent clause   An independent clause contains a subject, a verb and a complete thought (see p. 24). This is an independent clause:

Students complained to the professor.

This is not:

... that she didn't give them enough time to finish the exam.
(this is a dependent, or subordinate, clause)

Put together, we have what is called a complex sentence:

Students complained to the professor that she didn't give them enough time to finish the exam.

-ing endings A common suffix, *-ing* is added to a verb to create the present progressive form ("She is running for office.") or a verbal ("Running for office requires tenacity."). It can also be added to a noun, creating a verbal (a gerund) that gives the noun a sense of action. For example, *parenting* is the action of being a parent. Although "inging" a noun may occasionally create new words with distinct meanings, it can also be unnecessarily trendy.

Consider this example:

The boss believes in <u>gifting</u> her staff during the holidays.

This is an ugly, awkward construction. Use new *-ing* words sparingly and only when they capture a unique meaning without damaging the rhythm and sound of the language. See also the *-ize* entry.

in/into These prepositions are not interchangeable. *In* denotes location or position. *Into* indicates motion.

The photographer was already <u>in</u> the gallery when the star
(location, position)

witness was ushered <u>into</u> the courtroom.
(movement)

Regardless of current slang, *into* should never be used as a substitute for "involved with" or "interested in." This colloquial use is not only sloppy but also weak and ambiguous:

For the past year, she's been <u>into</u> swimming.
(ambiguous slang)

She's been swimming a mile a day for the past year.
(improved, with important detail)

initiate/instigate At our own instigation, we have initiated an investigation of this troublesome pair. When you mean that someone began or originated a contest, for example, it is *not correct* to write this:

He <u>instigated</u> the first sandcastle competition in Cannon Beach.

Actually, he *initiated* ("began") it. This would be a proper use of *instigate*:

She <u>instigated</u> the city's first recall campaign.

In this case she did not begin the movement—she pressed for it.

irregardless Strike this silly word from your vocabulary! *Regardless*, which means "without regard for" or "unmindful of" is what you're after. The *-less* suffix creates the negative meaning. If you add the *ir-* prefix, you create a double negative.

its/it's Once and for all, okay? *Its* is the possessive form of the neuter pronoun *it*. Do not confuse this with *it's*, which is a contraction for *it is* or *it has*:

The jury has reached <u>its</u> decision.
(possessive)

"<u>It's</u> time to decide this issue," he said.
(contraction of *it is*)

-ize words As a suffix, *-ize* has been employed since the time of ancient Greeks to change nouns into verbs (*final/finalize, burglar/burglarize*). But the "-ization" of words has reached epidemic proportions. We've been alarmed at the growing use of *incentivize*, for example. Writers interested in the clarity, precision and beauty of language need to take precautions. Tacking *-ize* onto nouns often creates useless, awkward and stodgy words. Will it get worse? Will we soon read something like this?

The agency may <u>permanentize</u> its position by <u>routinizing</u> its appointment procedures.

Before you use an *-ize* word, check your dictionary. Yes, our language is dynamic, but make sure the word has a unique meaning, and pay attention to its sound.

lay/lie *Lay*, a transitive verb form, always takes a direct object; *lie*, an intransitive verb, never takes a direct object:

Please <u>lay</u> the briefcase on my desk.
(dir. obj.)

The Galapagos <u>lie</u> in the Pacific Ocean, some 600 miles west <u>of Ecuador</u>.
(prep. phrase)

Be careful not to confuse *lie* and *lay* in the past tense. The past tense of *lie* is *lay*:

He finally <u>lay</u> down for a long winter's nap.

lend/loan Generally speaking, *lend* is a verb and *loan* is a noun. The one exception currently favored by most experts is *loan* as a verb in financial contexts:

The bank <u>loaned</u> the troubled firm $45 million.

This would be an appropriate use of *lend* as a verb and *loan* as a noun:

Don't <u>lend</u> him your car again, or you'll be applying for an auto <u>loan</u> before you know it.

less than/under If you mean "a lesser quantity or amount," use *less than*:

The county budget this year is <u>less than</u> $80 million.

If you mean "physically beneath," use *under*:

The zombies are waiting for you <u>under</u> the bridge.

linking verbs A linking verb connects a subject to an equivalent or related word in the sentence. That word—a predicate noun, a predicate pronoun or a predicate adjective—refers to the subject by either restating it or describing it. The principal linking verbs are *be, seem, become, appear, feel* and *look*.

She <u>became a best-selling novelist.</u>
(*Novelist*, a predicate noun—also called a *predicate nominative*—restates the subject *she*.)

It <u>is</u> he.
(*He*, a predicate pronoun, restates the subject *it* and stays in the nominative case. Yes, it does sound a bit formal, but ...)

Harold <u>feels</u> bad.
(*Bad*, a predicate adjective, describes the subject *Harold*.)

literal/figurative Considering these two words have opposite meanings, it's amazing that writers will substitute one for another. *Literal* means "word for word" or "upholding the exact meaning of a word":

This is a <u>literal</u> translation of "Beowulf."
Figurative, on the other hand, means "not literal; it is symbolic or metaphorical:

<u>Figuratively</u> speaking, she's on top of the world.

loath/loathe An errant vowel is all that stands between you and the adjective *loath* when you intend the verb *loathe*. *Loath* means "unwilling" or "disinclined."

I am <u>loath</u> to wake up before 10 a.m.
(The linking verb *am* joins the subject *I* with its adjective *loath*.)

But *loathe* is a verb that means "to dislike greatly."

Sandra <u>loathes</u> these early morning press conferences.

In case you think that this pair is the sole *h/he* duo, consider the noun *bath* and the verb *bathe*. Are there others? Time for a trip through the dictionary!

loose/lose *Loose* is an adjective denoting "unrestrained, unfixed or unbound," as in "loose shoes." *Lose*, a verb, means "fail to keep."

> **<u>Loose</u> lips are a plastic surgeon's dream.**

> **Don't <u>lose</u> your sense of humor!**

mantel/mantle Similar spellings and identical pronunciations aside, their meanings differ. A mantel is a shelf or ledge of sorts; a mantle is a cover. So:

> **He placed his grandmother's lace <u>mantle</u> over the fireplace <u>mantel</u>.**

may/might Both of these verbs indicate possibility, as in "I may go to the party tonight," but some usage experts contend that *may* indicates a stronger possibility than *might*. Our advice: stick with *may* unless the possibilities for action are extremely remote, as in this example:

> **I <u>might</u> as well be talking to the wall.**

mean/median Mean, an arithmetic average, is not the same as the median, which is the midpoint of a set of numbers. Here is a brief example using nine numbers.

> **Number of years spent on death row by prisoners of state X:**

Prisoner A 18	**Prisoner D 10**	**Prisoner G 6**
Prisoner B 14	**Prisoner E 7**	**Prisoner H 6**
Prisoner C 10	**Prisoner F 6**	**Prisoner I 4**

The median years spent on death row is seven; that is, half of the prisoners spent more than seven years in jail, and half spent seven years or fewer. The average (or mean) number of years spent on death row is nine; it is the sum of all the years (81) divided by the number of prisoners (nine).

modifiers These are words that enhance (modify) nouns, adjectives and verbs. Used properly, they provide description, as in

> **Brutus is a <u>shockingly</u> <u>intense</u> competitor.**
> (adverb)   (adjective)   (noun)

and

> **The turtle dove <u>cooed</u> <u>sweetly</u>.**
> (verb) (adverb)

Adjectives modify nouns; adverbs modify verbs and adjectives (see pp. 53–57) and **dangling modifiers**.

more than/over Like *less than* and *under*, these words are not interchangeable. Use *over* when you are referring to a spatial relationship. For figures and amounts, the correct phrase is *more than*:

More than 50 aircraft flew support missions over the desert.

none This indefinite pronoun often causes agreement problems. Use a *singular verb* when *none* obviously means "no one or not one." When *none* clearly indicates "no two, no amount or no number," use the *plural*. Don't be fooled by this plural object of the preposition—*none* is the subject:

None of the suspected rioters was arrested.
(not one rioter)

None of the taxes were paid.
(No taxes were paid.)

numerals Many organizations have specific style rules concerning numerals and a host of other issues. Check first; a stylebook may hold the answer. In the absence of other guidelines, however, follow these rules:

1. Spell out whole numbers below 10: *three, seven.*

2. Use figures for 10 and above: *14, 305.*

3. Spell out fractions less than one: *two-thirds, three-quarters.*

4. Spell out *first* through *ninth* when these words indicate a sequence:
She was <u>first</u> in line.
The <u>Ninth</u> Amendment came under scrutiny.
Use figures for *10th* and above.

5. Spell out numerals at the beginning of a sentence. The only exception is a calendar-year date.

There are also many guidelines for ages, percentages, fractions, election returns, monetary units, dimensions, temperatures and other specific cases. *The Associated Press Stylebook* is a good, comprehensive reference; *The MLA Handbook* and *The Chicago Manual of Style* are also widely used.

occur/take place *Occur* refers to "all accidental or unscheduled events"; *take place* refers to "a planned event":

The two flash mob gatherings occurred within 15 minutes of each other.

Your interview will take place at 2 p.m.

off of Be wary of prepositions that enjoy one another's company too much. They often practice grammatical "featherbedding"—having two do the job of one. *Off of* is one of those redundant, bulky constructions. *Off*, all by its lonesome, suffices.

<u>Get off</u> [of] my back!

Transit workers <u>walked off</u> [of] the job this morning.

one of the/the only one of the Subject–verb is not difficult when you identify the proper subject. When the subject is a pronoun (*who* or *that*, for example) and refers to a noun elsewhere in the sentence, the task is more challenging. Subject–verb agreement then depends on determining the correct antecedent. These guidelines should help.

1. In *one of the* constructions, the relative pronoun refers to the object of the preposition of the main clause, not the subject:

    Derek Jeter is <u>one of the</u> best ballplayers   who   have played the
    (subj.)   (obj. of prep.)   (pron.) (verb)
    game in the last 75 years.

You will note here that Jeter is not the only ballplayer who has played the game in 75 years. We are talking about many players who have played the game in that period.

2. In *the only one of the* constructions, the relative pronoun refers to the *subject* of the main clause:

    Will is the <u>only one</u> of the debaters who <u>writes</u> all his notes in
    (subj.)   (pron.)   (verb)
    cursive.

    In this sentence, the only cursive-writing debater is Will. Hence, the singular verb.

Did you notice the use of *who* rather than *that* in the two examples? Big difference—be sure to read the *that/who* entry.

ordnance/ordinance *Ordnance* is weaponry; it explodes, among other things. An *ordinance* (a law or regulation enacted by an elected body) can be politically explosive, but—well, you get the idea.

parallel structure Parallelism gives your writing clarity and order. It helps create balance and symmetry in addition to improving sentence rhythm.

Common errors in parallelism include mixing elements in a series, mixing verbals and switching voice. See pp. 80–81.

paraphrase This is a correct and concise summary of a direct quotation that may be too long or awkward to use. Accuracy is the key. In this example, the writer took a three-sentence direct quotation and put the essential information in one simple sentence, with proper attribution to the speaker:

> **According to District Attorney Adams, acceptance of the defendants' plea bargain will eliminate the need for a drawn-out and very expensive trial.**

Paraphrasing can create the wrong context or even change meaning, so the writer must be sure that the content of the paraphrase matches the essence of the quotation.

parentheses Parentheses add information within a sentence as a form of a smooth "aside" flowing within. Be careful not to overdo these, however. When you do use them, here is a simple rule concerning punctuation: Put the period *inside* the parentheses only if the parenthetical material is a complete sentence and can stand independently of the preceding sentence:

> **Don't fry that turkey in that tub of hot oil. (You'll be asking for trouble.)**

If the parenthetical material is essential to the main sentence, the period goes *outside*, ending the entire sentence:

> **The mourners chanted, "Vaya con Dios" ("Go with God").**

See pp. 101–102.

passive voice This is a generally ineffective and occasionally deceptive construction in which the subject of the sentence is actually the recipient of the verb's action. It adds words but diminishes clarity. Note the difference in directness and conciseness between these two examples:

> **The accounting scandal dubbed "Restatementgate" <u>by</u> journalists and commentators will be investigated <u>by</u> the Senate subcommittee.**
> (passive, in two constructions)

> **The Senate subcommittee will investigate the "Restatementgate" accounting scandal.**
> (active)

However, there are some suitable uses for passive voice (see p. 36).

people/persons Some editors contend that a group of human beings should be referred to as *people*, but individuals should be called *persons*. So, what is the scale of acceptable use for *persons*? Three? Six? We suggest you save yourself the headache—there are more pressing decisions in life. So if you are referring to one individual, you are referring to a person:

She's a wonderful <u>person,</u> don't you think?

If you are referring to more than one, use *people:*

Twelve <u>people</u> were arrested this morning in the jaywalking sting operation.

possessives Chapter 6 discusses the formation of possessives. This point, however, deserves emphasis: Possessives of personal pronouns are *not* the same as subject–verb contractions. Remember that the personal pronoun possessives *(my, mine, our, ours, your, yours, his, her, hers, its, their, theirs)* do not require an apostrophe. See the entry for *its/it's*.

poor/pore/pour Here's a challenging trio! *Poor* means "lacking," whether it's in health or wealth. But you *pour* a glass of juice in the morning before you *pore*, or "study attentively," over "When Words Collide."

precede/proceed To *precede* is to "come before," or to exist prior to," as in

The 9.0 magnitude earthquake <u>preceded</u> the devastating tsunami.

Proceed means "to go forward" or "carry on an action" (especially after an interruption).

After the cell phones stopped ringing, the conductor <u>proceeded</u> with the performance.

predicate The simple predicate of a sentence is the verb. The complete predicate includes the verb plus all its complements and modifiers.

I <u>read</u> "When Words Collide."
(simple pred.)

I <u>read "When Words Collide" with great enthusiasm</u>.
(complete pred.)

predicate adjective/predicate nominative A predicate adjective and a predicate nominative follow a linking verb. The predicate adjective modifies the subject, and the predicate nominative defines or restates the subject in different terms. Remember that a predicate nominative can be either a noun or a pronoun.

The movie's <u>plot</u> seems <u>weak.</u>
(subject)   (predicate adjective)

Her <u>dogs</u> are delightful <u>charmers.</u>
(subject)   (predicate nominative)

Predicate nominatives are obviously in the nominative case, as this pronoun demonstrates:

<u>It</u> was <u>she</u> who sounded the alarm.
(subj.) (pred. nom.)

preposition This hard-working part of speech links phrases, neatly tying a sentence into a coherent package:

The burglar was hiding <u>behind</u> the freezer.

In the example above, the preposition *behind* begins the prepositional phrase. Although a preposition can occasionally introduce a clause, it almost always precedes a phrase. When that phrase contains a pronoun, that pronoun must stay in the *objective case*:

Don't lay the blame on <u>us</u> reporters for this spate of bad news.

Avoid burdening a sentence with an unnecessary series of prepositions:

Dr. Flagranto followed his victim <u>through</u> the French doors <u>next to</u> the solarium, <u>with</u> the evil intent <u>of</u> murder <u>on</u> his mind.

Let prepositions enhance a sentence—don't let them drain the power of the verb!

prescribe/proscribe What a difference a single vowel can make! Those who **prescribe** are, in effect, setting something in motion in a directed or formal fashion. Examples:

The city council will <u>prescribe</u> bidding guidelines for the bridge project.

Dr. Singer <u>prescribed</u> an aggressive regimen of antibiotics for his patient.

To **proscribe**, however, is to forbid or to make illegal, as in

The new legislation <u>proscribes</u> four commercial lending practices that led to more than 100 bankruptcies in the past year.

principal/principle As a noun, *principal* refers to "someone who is first in rank or authority," such as the principal of a school. As an adjective, *principal* still means "first in rank or authority," such as the "*principal* reason for the levy's defeat." *Principle*, however, is only a noun. It means "a truth, doctrine or rule of conduct," such as "an uncompromising principle of honesty."

prone/supine   You're lying in the street, facedown. You're in a *prone position.* On your back? Now you're in a *supine* position. *Facedown* or *on your back* seems clearer to us—and easier to remember.

pronoun   Pronouns, working in place of nouns, change their form in the possessive (for example, *their* for *they*), which is why pronoun possessives don't need apostrophes. (And that's why the subject–verb contraction *it's* is not a pronoun!) Careless writers often position their pronouns indiscriminately, causing problems with antecedent identification:

> **<u>Pentagon briefers</u> tried to explain the field reports to the <u>journalists</u>, but it was apparent that <u>they</u> were hopelessly confused.**

See the problem? Be sure that antecedents are clearly identified (see pp. 70–71).

proved/proven   *Proved* is a verb. *Proven* is an adjective. This is a simple distinction, but some writers persist in using *proven* as part of a verb. Some dictionaries even list *proven* as an alternate verb form. We suggest you keep it simple. Examples:

> **The district attorney <u>has proved</u> the defendant's guilt beyond a reasonable doubt.**

In the example that follows, *proven* modifies the noun *track record.*

> **The district attorney has a <u>proven</u> track record for convictions.**

quotation marks   A quick briefing for you, for proper punctuation:

1. Periods and commas *always go inside* the quotation marks. Question marks and exclamation points go inside if they are part of the quoted material.

2. The most common error in quotation mark punctuation is in placement of the question mark. Two examples show its correct placement:

> **The senator asked the company president: "Can you honestly tell me that your baby food formula has never caused the death of a child in a Third World country?"**

The question mark belongs inside because it is part of a quoted question.

> **What did you think of "Avatar"?**

The entire sentence is a question; the movie title is not (see Chapter 7).

quotation/quote *Quotation* is a noun. *Quote* is supposed to be a verb. However, *quote* is often used as a noun these days. ("Get me some good quotes for this piece. It's dying of boredom.") Remember: *Quote* only accurate quotations!

real/really We're really serious about these real differences. *Real* is an adjective, and thus it can only be used to modify a noun. *Really* is an adverb; it can only modify adjectives. So, just to be clear: It would be *really* bad writing to say that you write *real* well. Got it?

reek/wreak They're both verbs, they sound similar, but their differences are real—really! *Reek* means to "emit or give off," as with an odor.

> **The meth lab <u>reeked</u> of noxious chemicals.**

Wreak means "to cause or inflict."

> **The tsunami <u>wreaked</u> havoc on the Vietnamese coast.**

rebut/refute It's easier to rebut a statement than to refute it. When you rebut a statement, you contradict it or deny it. But that doesn't mean you have conclusively proved the truth of your position. When you refute a statement, you have proved that you are correct. Use *refute* only if it is clear that the denial has been successful.

reluctant/reticent Don't be shy about enforcing this distinction. People who are *reluctant* to do something are not necessarily *reticent*. A *reluctant* person is unwilling to do something:

> **The board is <u>reluctant</u> to approve the merger.**

If a person is unwilling to speak readily or is uncommonly reserved, we generally describe that individual as *reticent*:

> **The professor has instituted a class for <u>reticent</u> speakers.**

renown/renowned *Renown*, a noun, means "fame or eminence"; *renowned*, an adjective, means "famous or celebrated":

> **Clarissa is a poet of great <u>renown.</u>**
> (noun—obj. of prep.)

> **Nobel laureate Linus Pauling was <u>renowned</u> for his**
> (pred. adj.)
>
> **groundbreaking work in chemistry.**

restrictive/nonrestrictive A restrictive clause is essential to the meaning of a sentence. Understanding this helps you in at least two ways:

1. The restrictive clause does not need to be set off by commas.

2. In a choice between *that* and *which, that* is always the correct pronoun subject or object for the restrictive clause.

> **The explosion <u>that</u> leveled two city blocks is still a mystery.**

A nonrestrictive clause, however, is *not essential* to the full meaning of a sentence. You must set off the clause with commas and use *which* instead of *that*:

> **Gifford's proposal, <u>which</u> would raise city taxes by an average of 12 percent, faces tough sledding in the council.**
>
> See also the entry for **that/which/who** on p. 181

run-on sentence Like the tedious infomercial, it doesn't know when to stop. Note how two complete sentences collide when an improperly placed comma can't stop the run-on:

> **Picket lines went up for a fourth straight <u>day, nurses</u> vowed to continue to honor them until contract talks resume.**

Use a semicolon instead of a comma, or insert the conjunction *and* after the comma to correct this fault. See also the entry for *comma splice.*

semicolon This punctuation mark helps you avoid the run-on sentence. When two independent clauses are in one sentence and are not separated by a conjunction such as *or, but* or *and*, they must be separated by a semicolon:

> **This is not your ordinary, barn-twirling <u>tornado; it</u> is the perfect storm.**

When two independent clauses are joined by a conjunctive adverb such as *however, nevertheless* or *therefore*, a semicolon also is needed before that adverb:

> **I can no longer justify our city's rapid budget growth; therefore, I have decided to resign as your mayor.**

The semicolon is considered a more formal mark of punctuation, and its use does create longer sentences. However, it is quite helpful in linking clauses that deserve such a connection.

sentence A sentence is one or more properly punctuated *independent* clauses that present a complete thought. Sorry to say, some writers do awful things to sentences: They make one run into another; they clutter them with unnecessary punctuation; and sometimes they neglect to put a verb in one but still call it a sentence:

Like this fragment.

A good sentence is an enlightenment, a forceful directive, an amusing bit of play. But it is always well-contained; its thought is always complete (see Chapter 3).

set/sit Normally the verb *set* requires an object:

Have you <u>set</u> the <u>agenda</u> for the annual meeting?
      (verb)   (dir. object)

Sit, however, *never* takes an object:

Please <u>sit</u> down for a few minutes.

See Appendix B to see how these and other irregular verbs change (are conjugated) according to their tenses.

since/because They are not synonymous. *Since* is needed to denote a period of time, whether continuous or broken:

It's been years <u>since</u> I've eaten meat.

Because gives a reason or cause:

His parents refused to co-sign the loan <u>because</u> of his unpredictable spending sprees.

In most circumstances, a comma is not needed before *because.*

split constructions The split infinitive is a frequent complaint of grammarians. However, the chief reason for objecting to the split infinitive—loss of clarity—is also the reason for avoiding unnecessary splits of a subject and a verb, and of a verb and its complement. Example:

The Secretary of Defense has agreed <u>to</u> before the start of the next Congressional session <u>reveal</u> the nature of troop buildups in the Gulf region.

In this sentence, insertion of two prepositional phrases between the two parts of the infinitive is both awkward and sloppy.

stanch/staunch *Stanch,* a verb, means to "stop or extinguish," as in

Surgeons struggled to <u>stanch</u> his sudden arterial bleeding.

Staunch, however, is an adjective that means "steadfast or true," as in

Buster has been a <u>staunch</u> friend through this nightmarish episode.

Note that some dictionaries cite *staunch* as an older variation of *stanch*. Let's underscore *older*—don't use older or secondary citations. They are there for historical context.

than/then *Then*—an adverb denoting time—is often confused with *than*. If you are comparing something, use *than*:

No one is more aware of America's breakfast habits <u>than</u> our fast-food franchise executives.

Then, on the other hand, carries the sense of "soon afterward":

Let's visit our favorite café and have caramel lattes; <u>then</u> we can head to the gym to suffer at the hands of our aerobics instructor.

Note that *then* cannot connect these two independent clauses on its own. A semicolon is needed.

When *than* is used to introduce an implied clause of comparison, the pronoun that may follow is most likely in the nominative case:

Tom is a lot smarter <u>than I</u> [am smart].

But some sentences won't permit this implied arrangement:

There is not a more dedicated volunteer <u>than her.</u>

"Than she is a volunteer" would not make sense here.

that/which/who As the entry for restrictive/nonrestrictive clauses says, *that* is used to restrict meaning and *which* is used to elaborate on it. These pronouns are used only in their particular types of clauses, but *who* can be used in both types when it refers to people or to things endowed by the writer with human qualities:

Recipes <u>that</u> require soy products are easy to follow.
(Restrictive—comma not needed)

Construction bonds, <u>which</u> can be a dependable tax shelter, carry different interest rates according to the credit standing of the local government.
(Nonrestrictive—gives explanation, and a comma is required.)

The demonstrators <u>who</u> interrupted the senator's speech were arrested.

(Restrictive—in this case, *who* is preferred over *that* because we are talking about real people, not inanimate objects or concepts. In this construction, a comma is not required.)

Newland, <u>who</u> is running for the state Senate seat from Medford, charged this morning that the governor's office has been "grossly mismanaged."
(Nonrestrictive—explanatory material follows *who*. Note the inclusion of commas.)

Reminder: People are who**s**, not that**s**!

their/there/they're   Here's a vexing trio. Although they are (*they're*) quite different, *their* (possessive) meanings are *there* for all to see.

So, *their* is the possessive form of the pronoun *they*:

Patrons are advised to keep a close eye on *their* valuables.

In the example above, the possessive pronoun *their* modifies *valuables*.

When it begins a sentence, *there* is called an expletive. It is sometimes called a false subject because it doesn't help determine the number of the verb:

<u>There</u> are many reasons to deny your petition.

In the above example, note that the noun *reasons*, not *there*, controls the number of the verb. As you could see from an earlier example, *there* can appear in other parts of a sentence.

They're is a contraction of *they* and *are*, used only informally when you want to combine subject and verb:

"<u>They're</u> coming to my party, aren't they?" she asked.
(Note position of the question mark inside the quotation marks.)

tortuous/torturous   The origin of these adjectives is the same, "to twist," but their usage is different. *Tortuous* connotes "twists and turns" and "complexity":

The <u>tortuous</u> road led to the fire lookout atop the mountain.
("twisted")

I can't make sense of your <u>tortuous</u> logic.
("convoluted")

Torturous is used in the context of its verb *torture*, "to inflict pain as a means of punishment."

His four days in the desert were a <u>torturous</u> experience.

TO-WH

toward/towards Dictionaries call *towards* "archaic and rare." Like backwards and forwards, towards is standard British usage. For your writing, just stick with *toward*.

try and/try to Avoid *try and*. It adds nothing but awkwardness. *Try to* does the job:

> She will <u>try to</u> talk with Coach Adams about her nagging injury.

unique This competent adjective is regularly adorned with superficial and redundant words, as in *most unique* or *very unique*. *Unique* means, simply, "the only one of its kind." Don't succumb to embarrassing overstatement.

up Up is anything but upbeat when it is coupled with a verb. Phrases such as *face up, slow up* and *head up* are clutter:

> He must <u>face up</u> to these challenges.

So—down with *up*! (See p. 112.)

very Be wary of *very* when you are tempted to give an adjective more punch. Don't overlook better, more precise adjectives and contribute to clutter. *Very* is but one example of an overused intensifier. Others are *really, completely, extremely* and *totally*. Rather than describe someone as very sad, you could choose among these words: *depressed, melancholy, sorrowful* or *doleful* (see p. 129).

waiver/waver A waiver (noun) is a document that relinquishes a right, whereas to waver (verb) is to waffle on a commitment, or to move or react unsteadily.

> The dean approved a <u>waiver</u> for their admission fees.

Waiver also has a verb form, *waive*, as in

> The dean agreed to waive all of Smith's late fees.

Pronunciation similarities aside, *waver* has a clear and distinct meaning:

> He never <u>wavered</u> on his commitment to the company.

who's/whose If you want to combine subject and verb, use *who's*:

> <u>Who's</u> making dinner tonight?
> (Who is making dinner tonight?)

If you need the possessive pronoun, use *whose*:

> <u>Whose</u> turn is it to make tofu burritos tonight?

who/whom Sloppy speech has done its best to eliminate *whom* from this handsome pair of pronouns, but the case for their proper use remains strong. The use of *whom* is not elitist; it is merely correct. *Whom* always is used as an object in a sentence. *Who* is always the subject. So:

<u>Who</u> will win the scholarship award?

Easy call. *Who* is the subject of the sentence.

<u>Whom</u> did you call first with your exciting news?

Yes, this takes a little more work to analyze, but the subject is *you* and the direct object is *whom*. You can quickly rearrange the sentence to understand this relationship:

<u>You</u> did call <u>whom</u> first with your exciting news.
(subj.)   (dir. obj.)

your/you're The same distinctions made in the entries for *their/there/they're* and *who's/whose* apply here. If you want to use the possessive form of the personal pronoun *you*, use *your*:

<u>Your</u> updated resume is impressive.
(*Your* modifies *resume*.)

If you want to compress (contract) the subject–verb *you are*, use *you're*.

Yes, <u>you're</u> going to be a great grammarian!

Homonyms, Homophones, Spell-Checks, Oh My!

Here is a great (or is that *grate*?) challenge to all who are far too (or is that *two*?) dependent on spell-checkers. These computer aids (not *aides*) won't help you with homonyms or homophones. We have seen spell-check actions lead to unintentional (and embarrassing) humor. More importantly, these mistakes threaten the precision and credibility of your writing.

These groupings should remind you of the importance of understanding the definitions and proper contexts for words. But first, two explanations:

A homonym is a word that has the same spelling and pronunciation as another word, as in *bear* (animal, a noun) and *bear* (a verb, "to carry").

A homophone has the same pronunciation but may have a different spelling, as in *moose* (animal, a noun) and *mousse* (a dessert, a noun).

Here is our priority list of more than 200 pairs—or trios—or even quartets! We won't focus on those with identical spellings, but the following, we hope, will make the point: Know the meaning of a word, no matter how it is spelled or pronounced.

accept	except
aid	aide
ail	ale
aisle	isle
all	awl
allowed	aloud
altar	alter
ascent	assent
assistance	assistants
aural	oral
away	aweigh
bail	bale
bare	bear

base	bass	
bazaar	bizarre	
beach	beech	
beat	beet	
berry	bury	
billed	build	
berth	birth	
bite	byte	
bloc	block	
boar	bore	
board	bored	
boarder	border	
bolder	boulder	
born	borne	
boy	buoy	
breach	breech	
bread	bred	
brake	break	
brewed	brood	
brews	bruise	
bridal	bridle	
brows	browse	
buy	by	bye
cache	cash	
cannon	canon	
canvas	canvass	
carat	carrot	caret karat
cast	caste	
cede	seed	
cell	sell	
cellar	seller	
censer	censor	sensor
cent	scent	sent
cereal	serial	
chance	chants	
chic	sheik	
chilly	chili	
choral	coral	
chord	cord	
chute	shoot	
cite	sight	site

clause	claws	
coarse	course	
colonel	kernel	
complement	compliment	
core	corps	
correspondence	correspondents	
council	counsel	
creak	creek	
cue	queue	
currant	current	
cymbal	symbol	
days	daze	
dear	deer	
desert	dessert	
dew	do	due
disburse	disperse	
discreet	discrete	
dual	duel	
earn	urn	
elicit	illicit	
ensure	insure	
ewe	yew	you
faint	feint	
fair	fare	
faze	phase	
feat	feet	
find	fined	
fir	fur	
flair	flare	
flea	flee	
flew	flu	flue
flour	flower	
for	four	fore
foreword	forward	
forth	fourth	
foul	fowl	
gait	gate	
gene	jean	

gorilla	guerilla	
grate	great	
groan	grown	
hair	hare	
hall	haul	
halve	have	
hangar	hanger	
heal	heel	he'll
hear	here	
heard	her	
higher	hire	
him	hymn	
hoard	horde	
hoarse	horse	
hole	whole	
holy	wholly	
hold	holed	
hour	our	
idle	idol	
in	inn	
incite	insight	
instance	instants	
its	it's **(see p. 51)**	
knead	kneed	need
knight	night	
knot	not	
know	no	
lay	lei	
leach	leech	
lead	led	
leak	leek	
lean	lien	
leased	least	
lessen	lesson	
levee	levy	
lie	lye	
links	lynx	

load	lode	
loan	lone	
locks	lox	
loot	lute	
made	maid	
mail	male	
main	mane	
maize	maze	
mall	maul	
manner	manor	
mantel	mantle	
marry	merry	
marshal	martial	
meat	meet	mete
medal	metal	mettle
might	mite	
mince	mints	
miner	minor	
missed	mist	
moose	mousse	
morn	mourn	
muscle	mussel	
naval	navel	
none	nun	
oar	or	ore
oh	owe	
one	won	
overdo	overdue	
overseas	oversees	
pail	pale	
pain	pane	
pair	pare	pear
palate	palette	pallet
passed	past	
patience	patients	
pause	paws	
peace	piece	

peak	peek	pique
peal	peel	
pedal	peddle	petal
peer	pier	
plain	plane	
pleas	please	
pole	poll	
poor	pore	pour
pray	prey	
presence	presents	
prince	prints	
principal	principle	
profit	prophet	
rack	wrack	
rain	reign	rein
raise	rays	raze
rap	wrap	
rapped	rapt	wrapped
read	red	
read	reed	
real	reel	
reek	wreak	
rest	wrest	
review	revue	
right	write	
ring	wring	
road	rode	rowed
roe	row	
role	roll	
rote	wrote	
rung	wrung	
rye	wry	
sail	sale	
scene	seen	
sea	see	
seam	seem	
seas	sees	seize
serf	surf	
sew	so	sow

shear	sheer	
shone	shown	
slay	sleigh	
soar	sore	
sole	soul	
some	sum	
stair	stare	
stake	steak	
stationary	stationery	
steal	steel	
straight	strait	
suite	sweet	
tail	tale	
taught	taut	
team	teem	
tear	tier	
tern	turn	
their	there	they're
theirs	there's	
threw	through	
thrown	throne	
tic	tick	
tide	tied	
to	too	two
toe	tow	
told	tolled	
vain	vane	vein
vale	veil	
vary	very	
vial	vile	
vice	vise	
waist	waste	
wait	weight	
waive	wave	
waiver	waver	
ware	wear	where
way	weigh	whey
weak	week	

weather	whether
we've	weave
wet	whet
which	witch
while	wile
whine	wine
who's	whose
wood	would

yore	your	you're

Irregular (Make That Troublesome) Verb Forms

Although your trusty dictionary gives you a proper spelling and a rank-ordered set of definitions, it also provides guidance to this important trio: a verb's present tense, its past tense and the formation of its past participle.

Why is this important?

Well, many verbs end in *-ed* in the past tense, as do their past participles, as in

I appear. (present tense)

I appeared. (past tense)

I have appeared. (past perfect tense)

However, as you look at this list of almost 100 groups of verbs in this appendix, you'll be reminded that the English language has a great number of what are called "irregular" constructions. For example, the present tense of the verb *leave* would not change to

He leaved the past behind.

As the list that follows shows, the past tense of *leave* is *left*.

What about go? The trio of tenses is **he goes, she went, it has gone**.

We hope this list is helpful, but please remember: Keep your dictionary nearby. Look it up, and be sure.

Present Tense	Past Tense	Past Participle (have/had)
arise	arose	arisen
awake	awoke	awaken
be	was, were	been
become	became	become
begin	began	begun
bleed	bled	bled
blow	blew	blown
break	broke	broken
bring	brought	brought
build	built	built
burst	burst	burst
buy	bought	bought
catch	caught	caught
choose	chose	chosen
come	came	come
cut	cut	cut
deal	dealt	dealt
dig	dug	dug
do	did	done
draw	drew	drawn
drink	drank	drunk
drive	drove	driven
eat	ate	eaten
fall	fell	fallen
feed	fed	fed
feel	felt	felt
fight	fought	fought
find	found	found
flee	fled	fled
fly	flew	flown
forbid	forbade	forbidden
forget	forgot	forgotten
forgive	forgave	forgiven
freeze	froze	frozen
get	got	gotten
give	gave	given
go	went	gone
grow	grew	grown
hang (to execute)	hanged	hanged
hang (to suspend)	hung	hung
have	had	had

hear	heard	heard
hide	hid	hidden
hold	held	held
hurt	hurt	hurt
keep	kept	kept
know	knew	known
lay	laid	laid
lead	led	led
leave	left	left
lend	lent	lent
let	let	let
lie	lay	lain
light	lit	lit
lose	lost	lost
make	made	made
meet	met	met
pay	paid	paid
quit	quit	quit
read	read	read
ride	rode	ridden
ring	rang	rung
run	ran	run
say	said	said
see	saw	seen
seek	sought	sought
sell	sold	sold
send	sent	sent
shake	shook	shaken
shine	shone	shone
sing	sang	sung
sit	sat	sat
sleep	slept	slept
speak	spoke	spoken
spend	spent	spent
spring	sprang	sprung
stand	stood	stood
steal	stole	stolen
stink	stank	stunk
swim	swam	swum
swing	swung	swung
take	took	taken
teach	taught	taught

tear	tore	torn
tell	told	told
think	thought	thought
throw	threw	thrown
understand	understood	understood
wake	woke	woken
wear	wore	worn
weave	wove	woven
win	won	won
wind	wound	wound
write	wrote	written

Index